Department of the Environment
Welsh Office

# Guidance on Safeguarding the Quality of Public Water Supplies

London    Her Majesty's Stationery Office

# Contents

Introduction

# Introduction

This document provides guidance on safeguarding the quality of public water supplies. It will be used as a reference document by the Drinking Water Inspectorate appointed by the Secretary of State for the Environment *and* the Secretary of State for Wales under Section 60 of the Water Act 1989 (HMSO 1989a) ('the Act'). Inspectors will be checking whether the various requirements concerning drinking water quality laid on water undertakers by relevant parts of the Act and the Water Supply (Water Quality) Regulations 1989 (HMSO 1989b) and the Water Supply (Water Quality) (Amendment) Regulations 1989 (HMSO 1989c) ('the Regulations') made under it are being met satisfactorily. Thus the document will be of major interest to water undertakers and to others with an interest in drinking water quality. However, it does not purport to offer any authoritiative interpretation of the Regulations. From time to time it will be updated.

Other documents of relevance include:

Reports on Public Health and Medical Subjects No. 71 'The Bacteriological Examination of Drinking Water Supplies 1982' (Report 71) (HMSO 1982a);

'Operational Guidelines for the Protection of Drinking Water Supplies' (Water Authorities Association/Water Companies' Association 1988);

'Guide to the Microbiological Implications of Emergencies in the Water Services' (Water Authorities Association 1985);

'Actions to minimise the Effects of Pollution Incidents affecting River Intakes for Public Water Supplies' (Water Authorities Association/Water Companies' Association 1984);

'Emergency Procedures on Pollution of Inland Waters and Estuaries' (National Water Council 1980);

Standing Committee of Analysts Methods (HMSO 1976 onwards);

World Health Organisation: Guidelines for Drinking Water Quality (WHO 1984);

Guidance letters issued by the Department of the Environment and the Welsh Office from time to time (see Annex 1);

and any subsequent revisions of these documents.

An explanation of the new legal regime in the Act and the Regulations relating to the quality of public water supplies is contained in a publication entitled, 'Drinking Water Quality in Public Supplies: An Explanation of the Water Act 1989 and the Water Quality Regulations 1989' (DOE 1989) prepared by the Department of the Environment. Copies may be obtained free of charge from the Drinking Water Division of the Department, Romney House, 43 Marsham Street, London SW1P 3PY.

The full titles of all documents referred to in this publication are provided in Annex 2.

# 1 Identification of Water Supply Zones

1.1 Water undertakers are required by Regulation 29 to prepare and maintain a record of water supply zones. As defined in Regulation 2 these zones are the basic units for establishing sampling frequencies, compliance with the standards and information to be made publicly available.

1.2 A reasonably consistent approach is needed in the selection of water supply zones, with sufficient flexibility being maintained for complex or unusual circumstances. Undertakers should therefore first identify whether an area is supplied from a single source or from more than one source. A source could be the outlet of a water treatment works, a borehole, a pumping station, a blending point or a service reservoir.

1.3 A single source which supplies a discrete area should always be recorded as a single water supply zone unless it normally serves a population greater than 50,000. In such circumstances the area must be sub-divided into water supply zones each with a population less than 50,000 (see definition of water supply zone in Regulation 2).

1.4 Any discrete area whether supplied by one or more sources should be sub-divided into separate supply zones if there are or could be significant differences in water quality within the area. Each zone would normally be served by an individual service reservoir or water tower, pumping or booster station, or would be distinguished as a separate pressure zone or by other appropriate features of the distribution system. In areas where the variations in water quality are complex or not predictable a convenient geographical boundary or an area served by an appropriate feature of the distribution system should be chosen to identify a water supply zone. Each zone should serve less than 50,000 people.

1.5 Temporary introduction of sources such as in an emergency or for limited periods during summer months should not influence the identification of water supply zones.

1.6 Each year, undertakers should review their delineation of water supply zones, although for year on year assessment of water quality the number of changes should be kept to a minimum.

# 2   Sampling Procedures and Identification of Sampling Points and Supply Points
(Parts IV and V of Regulations)

2.1 Part IV of the Regulations prescribes that water shall be sampled a certain number of times a year from points within the distribution system of each water supply zone chosen in such a way that, as far as is reasonably practicable, samples taken from those points are representative of the water quality in the zone as a whole.

2.2 The sampling points for lead, copper, zinc and at least 50% of the sampling points for microbiological parameters and residual disinfectant must be selected at random. For all other parameters the Regulations allow for a choice between random sampling and sampling at fixed points. Preferably, the points should be chosen at random because over time this is likely to provide the best picture of water quality. However if the water undertaker is satisfied that samples taken from certain fixed points are representative of the concentrations of one or more of these parameters in the water supply zone as a whole that parameter or parameters may be sampled at those fixed points.

**Sampling from random points**

2.3 Random sampling points should be predetermined using one of the following methods:

(a) consumers' taps in individual premises chosen at random from billing lists, electoral registers, post code lists or other similar and suitable lists; if access to the selected premises is not possible neighbouring premises could be chosen;

(b) locations consisting of groups of individual premises, such as a street or streets, post code or other similarly small geographical area chosen at random; the sampler chooses the individual premises within the location at which the sample is taken.

## Sampling from fixed points

2.4 Fixed sampling points should be predetermined and chosen in such a way that samples taken from them are representative, as far as is reasonably practicable, of the water quality throughout the zone. They should be changed only for good reason and then only at the start of a calendar year.

## Sampling for lead, copper and zinc

2.5 The sampling points must be chosen at random. The sample taken should consist of the first 1 litre of water which issues from the consumer's tap (random daytime sample). Each sample should be analysed for lead, copper and zinc.

## Sampling for microbiological parameters
### Consumers' taps

2.6 Taps connected directly to the main at consumers' premises provide the most satisfactory means of sampling water in a water supply zone. Preferably, samples should be taken from consumers' taps selected at random but where this is not practicable up to fifty per cent of samples in a water supply zone may be taken from fixed points. Where possible, samples should be taken from metal taps which are disinfected before sampling and which are sampled in such a way as to give representative samples of the water quality supplied to consumers' taps. Where only plastic taps or mixer taps are available they should be cleaned and disinfected before sampling. All external fittings such as anti-splash devices and hoses should be removed before sampling. Internal inserts should be removed where possible.

### Treated water leaving treatment works

2.7 Under Regulation 17, sampling is required from the point at which water leaves each treatment works. These points should be located so as to provide a representative sample of the water flowing into distribution. All treatment works outlets should be fitted with metal sampling taps of a hygienic design which do not have attachments or inserts and which are made from materials complying with BS 6920 (BSI 1988). Water should be supplied to the sampling tap through a sample line of a suitable material (if plastic, complying with BS 6920) which should be as short as possible.

Before a sample is taken, sample taps should be allowed to run for at least 2 minutes or as long as it takes to clear water standing in the sample line. Measurement of temperature can be used to determine when the standing water has been cleared.

*Service reservoirs and water towers*

2.8 Under Regulation 18, sampling is required from service reservoirs and water towers. Where reservoirs are divided into compartments, each compartment should be treated as a separate reservoir and sampled accordingly unless the compartments are inter-connected. Similarly, where there are 2 or more service reservoirs on a site, they should be sampled separately unless they are inter-connected. Preferably, all service reservoirs and water towers should have proper metal sampling taps, as described in 2.7, fitted at the outlet for sampling. Where it is impossible to provide a tap on site, a tap should be provided on the outlet main at the nearest possible point to the reservoir or tower. As an interim measure, pending provision of a proper sampling point, a consumer's tap (see paragraph 2.6) at a property fed directly from the outlet main should be used. Dip sampling should not be used for compliance sampling.

*Hydrants, meter boxes and standpipes*

2.9 When it is not possible to obtain a sample from a consumer's tap connected directly to the main and it is necessary to obtain a sample for operational or investigational purposes the sample may be taken directly from the main by means of a standpipe constructed for that purpose and attached to a hydrant or meter box on a flow-through main. The standpipe should be cleaned, stored and transported in a clean plastic bag, disinfected immediately prior to connection, flushed and then disinfected again. Flushing should be at a rate which avoids disturbance of deposits in the main. After use the standpipe should be cleaned and stored in a clean plastic bag.

**Authorisation of supply points**

2.10 Regulation 12 provides that the Secretary of State, upon written application of a water undertaker, may authorise sampling for certain specified parameters from a supply point (ie from a treatment works or a service reservoir) instead of from sampling points (ie consumers' taps) if he is satisfied that this is unlikely to produce significantly different data in respect of the parameters in question. Inspectors will need the following information when considering applications:

(a) a list of the relevant water supply zones and either the population supplied or the volume of water distributed ($m^3/d$) for domestic purposes in each zone;

(b) evidence that the concentration of the parameter in question does not change significantly between the supply point and the consumers' taps in the zones; or a reasoned scientific argument as to why there is unlikely to be any significant change in concentration in respect of the parameter in question; and

(c) in respect of trihalomethanes, evidence that the concentration is less than 20 µg/l at the supply point.

Such authorisation will not be possible for a zone in which blending of waters of different quality takes place unless the water undertaker can demonstrate with sufficient data that the different waters contain similar and relatively constant concentrations of the respective parameters.

**Sampling Procedures**

2.11 Regulation 21 sets out the general principles of sampling procedures to be applied.

*All parameters (except microbiological)*

2.12 Water undertakers should have set out in a sampling manual the procedures and precautions to be adopted for each parameter or group of parameters. As a minimum this should cover:

(a) the types of bottles or containers and their closures;

(b) the cleaning procedure for each type of bottle, container and closure;

(c) where appropriate, the amount and type of preservative to be added to ensure that there is no material change in water quality before analysis;

(d) the type of sample to be collected (eg first draw, flushed, stagnation) and the sequence for collecting samples for different parameters;

(e) the conditions of storage and transport (eg temperature) of samples; and

(f) the maximum time which can elapse before the analysis must commence.

2.13 Further general information on sampling procedures is given in the publications 'General Principles of Sampling and Accuracy of Analytical Results' (HMSO 1980a) and 'General Principles of Sampling' (HMSO 1989d). Detailed information for individual parameters or groups of parameters is given in the individual booklets in the series 'Methods for the Examination of Water and Associated Materials' published by the Standing Committee of Analysts (HMSO 1976 onwards).

*Microbiological parameters*

2.14 Water undertakers should have set out in a sampling manual the procedures and precautions to be adopted during sampling. As a minimum this should make clear that:

(a) the correct type of sampling bottles should always be used and bottles should not be used after their specified shelf-life;

(b) sampling bottles should be sterilised and used within a specified period and should contain sufficient freshly prepared sodium thiosulphate or other agent to neutralise any chlorine in the water to be sampled;

(c) scrupulous care should always be taken to avoid accidental contamination of the sample during collection;

(d) in general samples for microbiological examination should be collected before other samples unless there are other specific requirements (eg lead – see paragraph 2.5); and

(e) sample taps should always be cleaned and disinfected and the water run to waste for not less than 2 minutes before taking the sample for microbiological examination.

2.15 Samples should be kept cool using ice packs or equivalent when necessary and transported in the dark in sealed insulated boxes, which should be regularly cleaned and disinfected. Microbiological examination of

12

the water sample should be undertaken as soon as possible after collection. Every attempt should be made to start the examination within six hours of sample collection. Where logistics do not allow this, samples may be examined up to 24 hours after collection provided they are kept cool (2–10°C) and in the dark.

2.16 Further details of recommended sampling procedures are given in Report 71 (HMSO 1982), now being updated.

# 3 Sampling Frequencies
### (Regulations 13, 17 and 19)

**Situations when increased sampling frequencies apply**

3.1 Regulations 13 and 19 prescribe among other things that increased sampling frequencies shall apply when, as a consequence of a change in the treatment of water, an undertaker considers that a standard for a parameter has been or may be contravened. The following circumstances amongst others may give rise to this:

| *Examples* | *Parameters* |
|---|---|
| (1) any supply zone fed from a source where the treatment has been changed significantly. | parameters whose concentration alters during treatment, or which are present in coagulants eg aluminium or iron. |
| (2) any supply zone fed from a newly commissioned treatment works or an existing treatment works when a new process has been commissioned. | parameters whose concentration alters during treatment. |
| (3) any supply zone fed by a blend of sources where blending is designed to ensure compliance with a prescribed standard. | relevant parameters eg nitrate, fluoride. |
| (4) any supply zone in which mains re-lining has been carried out recently. | relevant parameters eg pH value and aluminium from cement mortar re-lining in areas with water of low alkalinity. |

**Authorisation of reduced sampling frequencies**

3.2  Regulation 13(6) provides that the Secretary of State may, upon written application of a water undertaker, authorise a reduced number of samples to be taken from consumers' taps in the calendar year 1990. The written application should include the following information:

(a)  the relevant water supply zones and either the population supplied or the volume of water ($m^3/d$) distributed for domestic purposes;

(b)  data for the parameter in question showing that in the previous three calendar years the requirements in Regulation 13(4) would have been satisfied in that period.

In assessing an application an Inspector should take into account all relevant material including the amount of data available and the difference between the actual concentrations or values and the prescribed concentration or value.

3.3  Regulation 13(5) allows for reduced frequencies in 1991 and 1992 provided that the Secretary of State is of the opinion that concentrations of parameters will not increase to a significant extent and has so notified undertakers. Similar information to that in the previous paragraph will be required to enable Inspectors to assess applications.

3.4  Regulation 17(4) provides that the Secretary of State may, upon written application of a water undertaker, authorise a reduced number of samples to be taken from water leaving treatment works in the calendar year 1990 for analysis for total and faecal coliforms and colony counts. Applications should include the following information to enable assessments to be made:

(a)  name of works and volume of water ($m^3/d$) normally supplied from the works;

(b)  evidence from the previous three calendar years which demonstrates an absence of total and faecal coliforms and no significant increase in colony counts;

(c)  information about the type of water treated at the works, for example, whether from upland or lowland surface sources, from springs or river gravels or from groundwater and the treatment given including details of the disinfection process.

In assessing an application the Inspector should take into account all relevant material including the amount of data available, the risk of coliforms being present in the treated water and the variability of colony counts.

## Operational sampling

3.5 For some parameters more frequent sampling and analysis, and in some cases continuous monitoring, will be needed for operational purposes at the treatment works.

## Individual parameters
*Fluoride*

3.6 Where fluoride is added to a water supply at the request of the health authority, the agreement between the water undertaker and the health authority will determine the sampling frequency. In most cases the agreement will accord with the Code of Practice on Technical Aspects of Fluoridation of Water Supplies (HMSO 1987).

*Pesticides*

3.7 Each water undertaker is required to develop a monitoring strategy for pesticides based on the likely risk of particular pesticides being present in the water source serving the zone. In developing a monitoring strategy water undertakers are advised to:

(a) assess as far as is practicable which pesticides are used in significant amounts within the catchment area; and

(b) assess as far as is practicable on the basis of the properties and method of use of these pesiticides, and local catchment knowledge, whether any of these pesticides are likely to reach a water source in the catchment area.

Information on pesticide use and properties is given in WP/18/1989 appended to this document.

3.8 On the basis of that strategy each water supply zone should be monitored at the frequency prescribed in Part IV of the Regulations for each pesticide identified as likely to reach that zone. Atrazine and simazine, which are widely used in non-agricultural situations, should be monitored in all water supply zones. Footnote (i) to Table 3 of Schedule 3 of the Regulations links the requirement to increase sampling and the permission to reduce sampling only to the particular pesticide concerned.

## Timing of sampling

3.9 For each parameter the specified number of samples should be taken in the water supply zone, at the treatment works and from service reservoirs at *regular* intervals throughout the year to detect any seasonal variations in water quality. In some circumstances water undertakers may need to take additional samples for some parameters for operational purposes to determine the extent of seasonal variations in water quality.

# 4 Performance Required of Analytical Systems
(Regulation 21)

## Non-microbiological parameters

4.1 Regulation 21(2)(d)(iii) specifies that the analytical systems and methods used should be capable of establishing within acceptable limits of deviation and detection whether the sample contains concentrations or values which contravene the standards.

*General specification of acceptable limits of deviation and detection of individual analytical results*

4.2 For most parameters, the maximum tolerable errors of individual analytical results are specified as follows:

(a) the maximum tolerable total error of individual results should not exceed C or 20% of the result, whichever is the greater;

(b) the maximum tolerable total standard deviation of individual results should not exceed C/4 or 5% of the result, whichever is the greater; and

(c) the maximum tolerable systematic error (or bias) of individual results should not exceed C/2 or 10% of the result, whichever is the greater,

where C = one-tenth of the prescribed concentration or value

and where the terms 'total error', 'total standard deviation', 'systematic error (or bias)' and 'limit of detection' have the meaning ascribed to them in 'The Chemical Analysis of Water, General Principles and Techniques', (Hunt and Wilson 1986).

4.3 This form of specification implies a limit of detection (4.645 times the within-batch standard deviation of results for blanks) equal to C, or one-tenth of the prescribed concentration or value.

4.4 Because of the nature of some parameters the above form of specification is not appropriate. Specifications for these parameters are given below.

*Odour*

Total error not more than ± 1 dilution number.

*Taste*

Total error not more than ± 1 dilution number.

*Temperature*

Total error not more than ± 0.5° Celsius.

*pH*

Total error not more than ± 0.2 pH units.
Total standard deviation not more than ± 0.05 pH units.
Systematic error not more than ± 0.1 pH units.
For water of conductivity less than 100 μS/cm these criteria are increased by a factor of 2.

*Dissolved or emulsified hydrocarbons and phenols*

Current methods are not capable of achieving a target total error of less than ± 20% for individual hydrocarbons or phenols. Laboratories are expected to use the best currently available methods, eg the methods published by the Standing Committee of Analysts. Further comments on the analysis for these parameters are made in paragraph 5.4.

*Trihalomethanes*

This parameter consists of the sum of the concentrations of four individual substances: trichloromethane, dichlorobromomethane, chlorodibromomethane and tribromomethane. For this parameter, for individual substances, C is one-fortieth of the prescribed concentration.

Current methods are not capable of achieving a target total error of less than ± 20% for many individual substances. Laboratories are expected to use the best currently available methods, eg the methods published by the Standing Committee of Analysts. Total pesticides should be regarded as the sum of the detected concentrations of individual substances. It is not possible to specify a total error requirement for total pesticides.

*Polycyclic aromatic hydrocarbons*

The prescribed concentration is the sum of the detected concentrations of six specified individual polycyclic aromatic hydrocarbons. It is not possible to specify a total error requirement for this parameter. For individual substances (except benzo 3.4 pyrene) C is one-fiftieth of the prescribed concentration. For benzo 3.4 pyrene C is 1ng/l.

**Microbiological parameters**

4.5 Good laboratory practice and analytical quality control are essential to achieve satisfactory results.

4.6 It is not possible to specify a performance for methods for microbiological parameters in terms of total error or limit of detection. However, the methods described in Report 71 (HMSO 1982) will be capable of the required performance. If alternative methods are used, they must be shown to be capable of producing equivalent or better performance by means of interlaboratory trials.

4.7 Any method used for the detection of indicator organisms must be capable of detecting the presence of small numbers of such organisms (even if they have been damaged in their environment or by the disinfectant), even as few as one in the appropriate sample volume, because false-negative results can have important consequences. Conversely, the methods used must be subject to good microbiological practice to ensure that contaminating organisms are not inadvertently introduced into the detection process. To avoid mis-identification of organisms, the methods used should be checked against standard reference procedures or against known strains of bacteria. Such strains should be selected and maintained in a manner that ensures their suitability for the purpose.

# 5 Analytical Methods
(Part II and Schedule 2 of Regulations)

**All parameters (except microbiological)**

5.1 In general, the methods published by the Standing Committee of Analysts in the series 'Methods for the Examination of Waters and Associated Materials' (HMSO 1976 onwards) will be capable of the performance required for determining compliance with the prescribed concentrations or values in the Regulations. However, laboratories must take steps to ensure adequate analytical quality control (see Chapter 6).

5.2 The prescribed concentration or value relates to the total amount of a parameter present in a sample (in solution and as suspended or collodial material) unless otherwise specified in paragraph 5.4 below.

5.3 There are some parameters in the Regulations that are difficult to determine or interpret because:

(a) analytical methods of adequate performance are not available;

(b) the parameter describes a group of substances; or

(c) the parameter is defined by an analytical method.

It follows from (c) that the analytical method must be used consistently by all laboratories.

Some other parameters may adequately include or represent another parameter or parameters, in which case determination of the representative parameter only is required.

5.4 The parameters which fall into these categories are set out in the following paragraphs together with recommendations and comments.

*Colour*

Determination of colour should be performed on samples which have been passed through a 0.45 μm filter. Visual comparison of colour intensity of samples against inorganic colour standards or calibrated permanent glass standards provides a direct determination of compliance with the prescribed value. An indirect method of measurement of the absorbance of the sample in 40 mm cells at a wavelength of 400nm using a spectrophotometer may be used; the absorbance reading has to be related to inorganic colour standards (Pt/Co) and this may be achieved by calibrating the spectrophotometer using such colour standards. The procedures described in the SCA methods (HMSO 1981a and HMSO 1988a) should be followed.

*Turbidity*

This parameter includes suspended solids which do not require separate measurement. Determination of turbidity should be performed by a method which measures turbidity as formazin turbidity units. These units are equivalent to Jackson turbidity units and to nephelometric turbidity units. The procedures described in the SCA method (HMSO 1981a) should be followed.

*Odour and taste*

The odour parameter includes hydrogen sulphide which does not require separate measurement. Odour and taste of water are closely linked. When water has an odour it almost invariably has taste; however an odourless water may have distinct taste. Determinations of odour and taste of water rely upon subjective assessments. Water undertakers are required to carry out frequent qualitative and less frequent quantitative determinations of odour and taste (Tables 1 and 2 respectively of Schedule 3 to the Regulations). The methods published by SCA (HMSO 1980b) should be used.

In the qualitative method the analyst smells or tastes a water sample at ambient temperature and classifies any odour or taste in terms of intensity and nature. This method will detect any chlorinous odours and tastes. Long-standing experience shows that consumers also assess qualitatively the odour and taste of their water supply for complaints about drinking water quality frequently concern odour or taste, particularly chlorinous odours and tastes. Water undertakers are expected to record all odour and taste complaints received from consumers. They are also expected to investigate persistent complaints and where practicable take appropriate remedial action.

The quantitative method involves the determination of the threshold odour or taste number. Only samples which have been dechlorinated should be used to determine compliance with the quantitative standards in the Regulations. The intensity of odour or taste is determined as a threshold number by each person on a panel of assessors. The threshold odour or taste number of the sample is the geometric mean of the individual results. This procedure reduces the subjectivity of the assessment. Because samples are dechlorinated before being tested the method measures any 'natural' or underlying odour or taste of the water and will not include most chlorinous odours or tastes. The quantitative odour determination has to be carried out in samples at 25°C to determine compliance with the standard in the Regulations and not at 40°C as recommended in the SCA method. A threshold odour or taste number obtained by the SCA method is converted to a dilution number (the unit of measurement given in the Regulations) by subtracting one. Thus a threshold number of 4 is equivalent to a dilution number of 3.

*Oxidisability*

This parameter is usually refered to as permanganate value (PV) or permanganate index (PI). The determination of PV or PI is empirical and many different procedures can be used. Therefore, the precise conditions of test have to be specified in order to define the parameter and to ensure comparability of results between laboratories. PV or PI is a measure of the amount of oxygen taken up from permanganate by an acidified and heated sample under the specified conditions of test. A procedure published by SCA (HMSO 1983), involving boiling for 10 minutes with 0.002M potassium permanganate, should be followed exactly. Other methods published by SCA (HMSO 1983) may also be valid, provided users have established a conversion factor.

*Kjeldahl nitrogen*

The analytical method has a limit of detection greater than the prescribed concentration of 0.1 mgN/l. Routine examination of samples for

Kjeldahl nitrogen is not required. If the analysis of a water sample shows unusually high colour, permanganate value or total organic carbon, analysts may carry out Kjeldahl nitrogen determination to assist in identifying the likely source of the increased amount of organic substances in the sample.

*Substances extractable in chloroform*

This parameter, which derives from the EC Drinking Water Directive, includes all substances extracted by chloroform under the conditions used in the analytical method. The method is non-specific as it does not identify the specific substances extracted. This parameter does not provide useful information about water quality hence routine examination of samples is not required.

*Dissolved or emulsified hydrocarbons*

This parameter includes all hydrocarbons extracted by petroleum ether. The analytical method has a limit of detection greater than the prescribed concentration of 10 μg/l. Routine examination of samples for dissolved or emulsified hydrocarbons is not required. However the presence of hydrocarbons in water is undesirable for aesthetic reasons. If hydrocarbons are present in significant quantities this may be apparent from the appearance of the water or from qualitative or quantitative tests for odour and taste. If hydrocarbons are thought to be present, the analyst may determine individual hydrocarbons (eg benzene and toluene, but not polycylic aromatic hydrocarbons) to assist in determining the origin of the hydrocarbons and any appropriate action that may be needed.

*Phenols*

This parameter includes all phenols. Phenols and their chlorinated derivatives can give rise to taste and odour. If the qualitative or quantitative tests for odour and taste suggest that phenols may be present the analyst may determine individual phenols (eg phenol, methyl phenols and chlorinated derivatives) to assist in determining the origin of the phenols and any appropriate action that may be needed.

*Surfactants*

This parameter is specifically concerned with substances reacting with methylene blue. The analytical method used should be based on complexation of the anionic surfactants with methylene blue in alkaline solution followed by extraction of the complex into chloroform and spectrophotometric determination. The method should be calibrated by standard solutions of lauryl sulphate or other specific anionic surfactants for which a conversion factor to lauryl sulphate has been established. The method published by the SCA (HMSO 1981b) is not based on lauryl sulphate and therefore a conversion factor is required.

*Dry residues*

This parameter is covered by the conductivity parameter and provided conductivity determinations are carried out on water samples, specific determination of dry residues is not necessary.

*Cyanide*

This refers to free cyanide and easily liberable cyanide. The method published by the SCA (HMSO 1988b) should be used.

*Ammonium*

This parameter is defined as the total concentration of free ammonia and ammonium ions. Most waters contain ammonia and ammonium ions in equilibrium with each other. The parameter is often referred to as ammoniacal nitrogen or total ammonium. One of the methods published by the SCA (HMSO 1980c) should be used.

*Phosphorus*

This refers to orthophosphates and acid hydrolysable polyphosphates and metaphosphates. The method published by the SCA (HMSO 1980d) should be used.

**Microbiological parameters**

5.5 The microbiological parameters included in the Regulations should be understood as having the following descriptions:

*Total coliforms*

Coliforms are members of a genus or species within the family Enterobacteriaceae, capable of growth at 37°C, and normally possessing β-galactosidase.

*Faecal coliforms*

Faecal coliforms are thermotolerant coliform organisms which are capable of growth and of expressing their fermentative properties at 44°C.

*Faecal streptococci*

Faecal streptococci are Gram-positive cocci, forming pairs and/or chains which are non-sporing, oxidase and catalase negative, possess Lancefield's Group D antigen and can hydrolyse aesculin. They can grow under aerobic and anaerobic conditions in the presence of bile salts and in concentrations of sodium azide which are inhibitory to coliform organisms and most other Gram-negative bacteria.

*Sulphite-reducing clostridia*

Sulphite-reducing clostridia are Gram-positive, anaerobic, spore-forming rods which reduce sulphite to sulphide. This group is typified by *Clostridium perfringens* which produces a stormy fermentation in milk. The standard for sulphite-reducing clostridia is 1 organism or less in a 20ml sample examined using a multiple tube method. Report 71 includes a multiple tube method and a membrane filtration method both of which estimate the number of organisms in a 100ml sample. A result of 5 organisms or less in 100ml of sample obtained by either method is regarded as equivalent to 1 organism or less in a 20ml sample.

5.6 The methods for examination of the organisms described in paragraph 5.5 should be those described in Report 71 (HMSO 1982) and any subsequent revisions. Where daily sampling of water leaving treatment

26

works is required, test kits, which determine simply whether an indicator organism is present or absent in 100 ml of sample, may be used for one or two sampling occasions per week but no more. If the test kit indicates the presence of an indicator organism the procedures set out in paragraph 7.7 should be followed and any further samples examined using the standard methods described in Report 71.

*Pathogenic and other organisms*

5.7 For technical and epidemiological reasons, the direct search for pathogenic bacteria or other pathogenic micro-organisms such as viruses and cryptosporidia has no place in the routine microbiological examination of water supplies. There are occasions, however, when an investigation for faecal pathogens may be necessary – for example, when a water supply is suspected of transmitting disease. In such cases there must be close liaison with relevant officers of the appropriate local authorities, the medical officer with responsibility for environmental health and the Public Health Laboratory Service to ensure that efforts are directed to the most likely causal organisms. Amongst the organisms which may need to be sought by a competent laboratory service are salmonellas, shigellas, cryptosporidia, campylobacters, giardia, aeromonads, enteric viruses, vibrios, and pathogenic amoebae. Water policy letters WP/6/1989 and WP/15/1989 (see Annex 1) give advice on cryptosporidia.

# 6 Analytical Quality Control
(Regulation 21)

6.1 Regulation 21(2)(e) specifies that any laboratory analysing samples to determine compliance with the standards prescribed in the Regulations should have a system of analytical quality control that is periodically subjected to checking by a person approved by the Secretary of State. Departments are still considering the procedure whereby a person can be approved for this role and will advise water undertakers in due course.

**Non-microbiological parameters**

6.2 For internal quality control, laboratories are expected to carry out the following procedures in sequence and obtain satisfactory results before using any analytical system to determine compliance with the standards prescribed in the Regulations:

(a) Select an analytical system capable of achieving results of the required accuracy for the parameter in question (see Chapter 4). The analytical method to be followed must describe unambiguously and in sufficient detail, the full analytical procedure.

(b) Estimate the within-laboratory total standard deviation of individual analytical results for blanks, standard solutions, samples and spiked samples having concentrations over the range of interest (including the prescribed concentration), over at least five batches on five separate days. Each estimate of total standard deviation should have at least ten degrees of freedom.

Simultaneously, assess the recovery of added 'spikes' of the parameter concerned from typical samples, in order to check certain sources of bias. The samples to be spiked should have low concentrations, in relation to the prescribed concentration, and the spiked samples should have concentrations close to the prescribed concentration.

The estimates of total standard deviation must not be significantly greater at the 95% level than the specified maximum tolerable total standard deviation at the relevant concentration. The recovery of added spike should not be significantly less than 95%, or significantly greater than 105%. If these conditions are not met, the cause must be found and rectified and the tests repeated. References should be consulted for further details of the tests and the treatment of their results (Cheeseman and Wilson 1978; Hunt and Wilson 1986; HMSO 1980a and HMSO 1989). In some cases, particularly for organic parameters with low prescribed concentrations, it may not be possible to meet the recovery target for added spike; the currently available technique which gives closest recovery to this target should be used.

(c) Set up a quality control chart to maintain a continuing check on analytical performance when the system is in routine use. As a minimum, the control analysis should be of a standard solution having a concentration close to the prescribed concentration for the parameter in question. Any problems revealed by the control chart should be immediately investigated, and remedial action taken. References should be consulted for further details.

The results of both the preliminary tests and the control charts should be available for inspection.

6.3 Laboratories will also be expected to participate in external quality control schemes where available, involving the distribution of check samples. The results should be available for inspection. Any evidence obtained by such participation showing that analytical errors exceed those specified in Chapter 4 for the parameter in question should trigger immediate investigation and remedial action. The form of such investigation and action will depend on individual circumstances. However, for parameters which give rise to continuing problems in meeting the accuracy requirements and whose levels approach the prescribed concentration, laboratories may need to conduct detailed development work on their analytical system, and more detailed analytical quality control.

**Microbiological parameters**

6.4 It is necessary for successful microbiological examinations to be able to demonstrate the presence or absence of a particular class of micro-organism in a given sample volume and to estimate numbers. The detection of small numbers of organisms is particularly important. Currently recommended methods require culture of the organism to achieve detection so the culture medium used must be shown to be capable of supporting the growth of the appropriate organism. Because of the ubiquitous nature of most microbes, it is essential to ensure that any that are detected have originated from the original sample and have not been introduced inadvertently during sampling or in the laboratory.

6.5 Internal quality control demands that as a minimum –

(a) All equipment, glassware, sampling bottles etc. must be sterilized. The methods and equipment used for this purpose must be regularly checked to ensure that sterilization can be achieved. It is not sufficient to rely on autoclave tape as an indicator of sterility.

(b) All media and reagents must be sterile and every batch of completed culture medium must be checked for sterility before use.

(c) Media must also be checked to ensure that each batch will support the growth of the organism to be detected. In addition, selective media should be checked to ensure that the growth of unwanted organisms is minimised.

(d) All media and reagents must be stored under conditions that ensure that deterioration does not occur. Media and reagents that have exceeded their 'shelf-life' must be discarded.

(e) Incubators should be fan-assisted and temperatures must be checked each day of use, both during incubation and when unloaded.

(f) Procedures must be followed that will ensure that all cultures and subcultures etc are clearly identified with the original sample.

(g) Appropriate records should be kept to ensure that all necessary procedures have been followed during the examination of a particular sample or set of samples.

(h) The regular examination of samples containing a known organism will provide an additional check on the performance of the methods used. For example a positive control which contains thermotolerant and non-thermotolerant coliform organisms, such as natural water known to contain the organisms or a water to which reference organisms have been added, should be included with each batch of samples and the results recorded.

6.6 Laboratories will also be expected to participate in external quality control schemes, where available, involving distribution of check samples. Any evidence obtained by such participation showing deficiencies in the procedures should trigger immediate investigation and remedial action.

6.7 As accurate laboratory results are dependent upon the quality of the received sample, the appropriate technique for obtaining a suitable sample must be strictly adhered to (see paragraphs 2.6–2.9 and 2.14–2.16).

# 7  Action if Quality Standard Infringed
(Part II of Regulations)

7.1 Water undertakers have given a number of undertakings under Section 20(5)(b) of the Act to take particular steps to secure or facilitate compliance with the quality standards where they are being infringed. The Departments have also granted a number of relaxations of some of the standards under Regulation 4, some of which are time limited. Undertakings and relaxations afford undertakers relief from enforcement action under Section 20. However there will be other situations, not covered by an undertaking or a relaxation, where a sample is taken indicating an infringement of a standard. This chapter provides guidance on the action to be taken by the undertaker in such situations.

7.2 For most parameters standards apply to each sample taken. If a standard is infringed, that water is unwholesome unless a relaxation has been given. This does not necessarily mean that water in the whole supply zone is unwholesome or even that water at the point where the sample was taken remains unwholesome. Only further sampling will determine that. This is relevant to the Secretary of State's obligation to take enforcement action where he is satisfied that a standard is continuing to be infringed or that it was infringed and it is likely to be so again (Section 20(1)). It is also relevant to his consideration of whether an infringement of a standard is 'trivial' and therefore whether he may disregard it under Section 20(5)(a).

7.3 If an undertaker is not clear whether an infringement falls within the terms of the previous paragraph, it should consult the appropriate Department. The procedure set out in Table 7.1 should be followed as a general guide in the event of an infringement of any standard. In addition the following action should be taken in relation to the circumstances specified.

**Any significant water quality failure**

7.4 A 'significant' failure cannot be defined, but examples of microbiological and chemical failures are given in paragraphs 7.8, 7.9 and 7.12. When

32

significant failures occur there should be a presumption that water in supply is a potential health hazard, in which case water undertakers should immediately obtain expert advice. Speed will be of the essence so it follows that water undertakers must have standing arrangements for obtaining expert advice on toxicological and microbiological matters either from individual experts or from centres of expertise. When such an incident occurs water undertakers will be expected to –

(a) Take all reasonable steps to rectify the situation and get supplies back to normal as soon as possible.

(b) Take action to protect consumers which may include:

switching to temporary alternative supplies or providing suitable alternative supplies for particular groups such as babies;

continuing supply but advising consumers not to use water for drinking and cooking, or to boil water for such purposes;

shutting off the supply and providing water by tanker;

issuing advice to all water users; and

providing information to press and local radio.

(c) Notify relevant officers of the local authorities and district health authorities in accordance with agreed procedures (Regulations 30(5) and (6) and 33(1)(a)) and consult with regard to the appropriate steps being taken and to be taken. This notification should be carried out without delay, and should extend to incidents which are likely to cause alarm to consumers owing to changes in taste or appearance of the water, as well as ones which might directly affect their health.

(d) Carry out increased operational monitoring according to the nature and seriousness of the incident and keep separate records of all such monitoring and action taken during the incident.

(e) Consider whether an application should be made to the appropriate Department for an emergency relaxation under Regulation 4(1)(a).

7.5 If any such incident could involve significant health risks to consumers the Department of the Environment or Welsh Office should be notified as soon as possible in accordance with agreed procedures.

**Any standard infringed owing to fittings in ownership of consumer**

7.6  Where a standard is infringed solely because of the state of fittings in the ownership of a consumer, the water undertaker will inform the consumer so that he may take remedial action. When there is a significant health risk the local authority would also be informed in accordance with agreed procedures.

**Microbiological standard infringed**

7.7  Further investigation has to be instigated the same day when 'presumptive' coliforms are detected in any sample taken from treatment works, service reservoirs, water towers or consumers' taps. As a minimum this should include:

(a)  examination of a further sample from the same location as the original sample and samples from related points (this may include examination for a wider range of organisms such as faecal streptococci and clostridia);

(b)  appropriate tests on the presumptive colonies of the original sample to confirm or otherwise the presence of coliforms or faecal coliforms; and

(c)  where appropriate, immediate checks on:

i. the operation of the treatment works eg failure of filtration or disinfection;

ii. contamination of the distribution system through eg burst mains, leaking service reservoir, backsiphonage, loss of pressure or cross connections;

iii. contamination of raw water at source; and

iv. the sampling tap and sampling and laboratory procedures.

No further action is necessary if the investigation at (b) does not confirm the presence of coliforms or faecal coliforms but the results of the additional operational samples and checks should be recorded.

7.8  If these investigations show evidence of actual or potential microbiological contamination, then effective remedial action should be instituted immediately to ensure that satisfactory microbiological conditions are restored. This is particularly important if large numbers of coliforms or any faecal coliforms are detected. The action will depend on local circumstances but it could include, where appropriate:

(a) increasing the disinfectant dose at the treatment works or in the distribution system;

(b) correcting the operation of treatment works including filtration and disinfection;

(c) cleaning, flushing or disinfecting mains and service reservoirs;

(d) isolating and then correcting any identified source of water contamination; and

(e) protecting raw water sources.

In some cases the remedial action may be of a short-term nature pending the completion of longer term measures.

7.9 If any evidence is detected of actual or potential serious microbiological contamination, such as high counts of faecal coliforms, the presence of specific pathogens or failure of the disinfection or filtration processes, then urgent action must be taken including that specified in paragraph 7.4.

7.10 If intermittent and related low-level failures for total coliforms are detected anywhere in the system (for example failure when there is heavy rain or failures in the same place at the same time each year) water undertakers should establish the cause and take remedial action. Remedial action must be taken in respect of each zone where more than 5% of samples contain coliforms (Regulation 3(6)) and where a similar degree of non-compliance is found at a service reservoir or water tower. Such programmes of remedial action should be submitted as soon as possible to the Department of the Environment or the Welsh Office as appropriate in the form of an undertaking under Section 20(5)(b) of the Act.

7.11 Continuous review is needed of colony counts in routine samples taken from treatment works, service reservoirs and water supply zones. Further investigation and, where appropriate, remedial action should be taken when:

(a) there is a sudden and unexpected increase in a colony count, particularly the 37°C count, compared with that normally found in the particular water supply; and

(b) there is a significant trend of increasing colony counts in the supply over a period of a few years.

## Chemical standard temporarily infringed owing to emergency or operational difficulties

7.12 Short-term infringement of standards may occasionally occur because of operational difficulties at a treatment works or in the distribution system or following a pollution incident. Examples are:

(a) pump/power failure at treatment works;

(b) other mechanical failure eg dosing pumps;

(c) flooding of treatment works;

(d) fire/explosion at treatment works;

(e) failure of pump or main burst leading to loss of blending capacity in distribution;

(f) disturbance of mains deposits due to burst or excessive water use by fire brigade;

(g) chemical spillage affecting a water source; and

(h) sudden, exceptional, unexpected changes of raw water quality.

In the event of any of the above or similar occurrences the water undertaker should take the action specified in paragraph 7.4.

## Chemical standard infringed regularly or chronically

7.13 If a standard is infringed in any of the following circumstances, unrelated to emergencies, operational difficulties or a specific pollution incident:

(a) because of the characteristics of the raw water arising from the nature and structure of the ground in the catchment;

(b) because of exceptional meteorological conditions;

(c) because a regular, intermittent or chronic failure to comply is due to the state of the treatment works or distribution system; or

(d) because of activities in the catchment area giving rise to diffuse pollution;

to avoid enforcement action under Section 20 of the Act, a water undertaker should either seek a relaxation under Regulation 4 or should offer an undertaking under Section 20(5)(b) to take appropriate steps to secure or facilitate compliance.


**Pesticide standard infringed**

7.14 The maximum admissible concentration for this parameter in the EC Directive was set to minimise the occurrence of pesticides in drinking water and is not based on toxicological evidence. The Government is pressing the European Commission for a review of the pesticide parameter. Advisory values have been calculated in the UK for some pesticides from published toxicological data and with a wide margin of safety. The current values are set out in WP/18/1989 (Annex 1), where their derivation and significance are explained. They will be reviewed as new evidence becomes available. The values are reproduced in Table 7.2.

7.18 The advisory value for aldrin/dieldrin is lower than the standard in the Regulations. If such a value is exceeded in a supply but the standard is not infringed the undertaker should treat the matter on the same basis as paragraph 7.4 and also consult the appropriate Department on measures to be taken.

7.19 Each year, water undertakers will be asked to provide:

(a) information to the NRA and the Department of the Environment or Welsh Office on pesticide concentrations which exceed the standard; and

(b) a report to the appropriate Department on the extent of pesticide contamination of water supplies for the Government to take into account in considering national regulation of pesticides.

This information will most appropriately be provided at the same time as the annual report required by Regulation 31 is published.

**Standard infringed for other reasons**

7.20 Occasional infringements of standards may occur which are not covered by the preceding paragraphs. In these cases the procedure set out in the relevant parts of the Table 7.1 should be followed.

7.21 Increased programmed sampling should be instigated in accordance with the criteria set out in the Regulations.

**Emergency procedures**

7.22 It is important that water undertakers have written contingency arrangements to deal with emergencies. All staff should be familiar with them and procedures should be rehearsed from time to time. Each undertaker should review its arrangements regularly to ensure that they are up-dated to take account of its own emergencies and those that affect other undertakers so far as details become generally known. Hazard study techniques should be considered, if this has not been done already.

7.23 Undertakers should refer to the following documents on emergencies and implement their recommendations where relevant:

Guide to the Microbiological Implications of Emergencies in the Water Services (WAA 1985);

Action to minimise the Effects of Pollution Incidents affecting River Intakes for Public Water Supplies (WAA/WCA 1984);

Emergency Procedures Pollution of Inland Waters and Estuaries (NWC 1980); and

Guidance for dealing with Incidents and Emergencies involving the Release of Radioactivity to the Environment (DOE 1987).

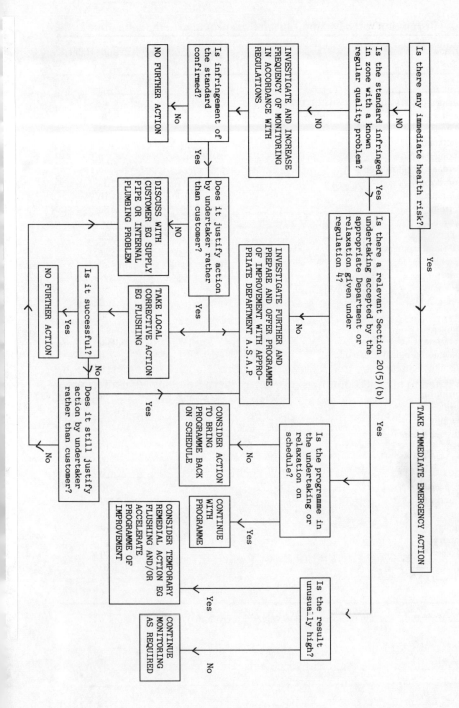

Table 7.1 PROCEDURE TO BE FOLLOWED IN THE EVENT OF A STANDARD BEING INFRINGED

39

*Table 7.2* Advisory Values for some Pesticides*

| Pesticide | Advisory Value µg/l |
|---|---|
| Aldrin and dieldrin | 0.03 |
| Atrazine | 2 |
| Bromoxynil | 10 |
| Carbendazim | 3 |
| Carbetamide | 500 |
| Carbophenothion | 0.1 |
| Chlordane (total isomers) | 0.1 |
| Chloridazon | 50 |
| Chlormequat | 10 |
| Chlortoluron | 80 |
| Clopyralid | 100 |
| 2,4–D | 1000 |
| DDT (total isomers) | 7 |
| Dicamba | 4 |
| Dichlorprop | 40 |
| Difenzoquat | 80 |
| Dimethoate | 3 |
| EPTC | 50 |
| Gamma HCH | 3 |
| Glyphosate | 1000 |
| Heptachlor/heptachlor epoxide | 0.1 |
| Hexachlorobenzene | 0.2 |
| Ioxynil | 10 |
| Isoproturon | 4 |
| Linuron | 10 |
| Malathion | 7 |
| Mancozeb (maneb plus zinc oxide) | 10 |
| Maneb | 10 |
| MCPA | 0.5 |
| MCPB | 0.5 |
| Mecoprop | 10 |
| Metamitron | 40 |
| Methoxychlor | 30 |
| Paraquat | 10 |
| Prometryn | 10 |
| Propazine | 20 |
| Simazine | 10 |
| Triadimefon | 10 |
| Triallate | 1 |

* The derivation and significance of these values are given in WP/18/1989 (Annex 1)

# 8   Action where Risk of Water becoming Unwholesome after leaving Undertakers' Pipes
(Regulation 24)

8.1 Under Regulation 24, a water undertaker has certain duties relating to the supply of wholesome water when there is a risk that the water may not comply with the standards for lead, copper or zinc after it has left the undertaker's pipes and passed through lead, copper or galvanised iron pipes on consumers' premises. Whenever practicable, a pH value greater than 6.5 should be maintained in the water delivered to consumers, so that the water is not unduly aggressive towards these plumbing materials.

**Lead**
*Risk that water supplied fails to comply with the standard.*

8.2 Regulation 24(1) refers to the risk that the water may cease to comply with the standard for lead of $50\mu g/l$ after leaving the water undertaker's pipes. Water undertakers should assume that there is a risk of a failure to meet the standard for lead in samples taken from consumers' taps in *all* their water supply zones, unless evidence is available that there is no such risk. In many zones this evidence of no risk will already be available from previous monitoring programmes in which random daytime samples (the first water which issues from the tap at any time during the day) have been taken from randomly selected properties supplied through lead pipework. The evidence should be derived from a minimum of 20 samples, but preferably 50 samples or more, taken regularly throughout a period of at least 1 year with a relevant proportion of samples having been taken during the summer months when water temperatures are at their highest and lead concentrations are likely to be at a maximum. If all such samples taken in a water supply zone are shown to comply with the 50 $\mu g/l$ standard the water undertaker may assume that there is no risk of exceeding the lead standard in that zone. If previous monitoring programmes are not adequate to provide sufficient evidence, it may be obtained by carrying out before 30 June 1991 a survey over a period of at least 1 year in which a minimum of 20 samples, but preferably 50 samples or more, are taken in a water supply zone.

8.3 Where a risk has been identified, all water of low alkalinity (less than about 50 mg $CaCO_3$/l) should have pH adjustment and control to maintain a pH value at or near to 8.5 and preferably not below 8.0 at consumers' taps, as this will bring about a significant reduction in lead concentrations (Lead in Potable Water, Technical Note No 5, DOE 1984). Water undertakers should determine whether a further significant reduction in lead concentration could be achieved by additional treatment of the water, for example by dosing with an orthophosphate. For waters of alkalinity greater than about 50 mg $CaCO_3$/l, water undertakers should determine whether a significant reduction in lead concentration could be achieved by water treatment, for example by pH adjustment and control or by the addition of an orthophosphate.

8.4 The effectiveness of treatment in achieving a significant reduction may be determined for example by testing the water in an on-site rig using 2 metre lengths of conditioned, new lead pipe. (Guidance on the construction and operation of a rig is in preparation and Departments will advise water undertakers of its availability in due course.) In this test, the concentration of lead is determined in water samples taken from the rig before and after the proposed treatment. The test rig is designed so that the samples taken represent water which has been in contact with the pipe for 30 minutes. Alternatively, the effectiveness of treatment may be determined in a field trial carried out in a small part of a zone whereby lead concentrations in 30 minute stagnation samples taken from consumers' taps are measured before and after the introduction of treatment.

8.5 Where a risk has been identified, water undertakers should submit undertakings under Section 20(5)(b) to investigate whether a significant reduction in concentrations could be achieved by a reasonably practicable treatment and, if so, to install treatment as soon as practicable.

*Treatment unlikely to achieve significant reduction*

8.6 Regulation 24(4)(a) does not require an undertaker to treat water in any zone where treatment is unlikely to achieve a significant reduction in lead concentration. To provide some consistency in deciding whether a significant reduction would be achieved, the following guideline should be used. As a general rule, a reduction of 30% or more with a minimum reduction of 10 µg/l in the average lead concentration in 30 minute stagnation samples taken from the test rig or consumers' taps may be regarded as a significant reduction in the concentration of lead following the treatment. For example, if the lead concentration before treatment is 60 μg/l, a reduction to 42 μg/l or lower concentration after treatment would be regarded as significant, and if the lead concentration before treatment is 20 μg/l a reduction to 10 μg/l and not to 14 μg/l would have to be achieved to be regarded as significant.

*Risk relates to an insignificant part of zone*

8.7 Regulation 24(4)(b) does not require an undertaker to treat water in any zone where the prescribed risk relates only to water supplied in an insignificant part of the zone. Where less than 5% of the total population or, in any case, not more than 1000 people (approximately 400 properties) in the zone are supplied through lead pipes, the risk may be regarded as relating to an insignificant part of the zone.

8.8 The risk may also be regarded as relating to an insignificant part of the zone when either:

i. between 20 and 50 random daytime samples have been taken and no more than one sample has exceeded the lead standard; or

ii. more than 50 random daytime samples have been taken and less than 2% of samples have exceeded the lead standard; and

iii. the cause of the failure or failures was recently installed copper pipes joined with a lead based solder or it was peculiar to a property or properties and was unlikely to be repeated elsewhere in the zone eg a property supplied through a long length of lead pipe.

8.9 For any zone with less than 250 population (approximately 100 properties) the water undertaker should consider whether it would be more practical to promote a policy of lead pipe replacement whereby the water undertaker replaces its part of the lead service pipe and the householder replaces the remainder of the service pipe than to treat the water passing into that zone.

*Treatment not reasonably practicable*

8.10 Regulation 24(4)(c) does not require an undertaker to treat water if treatment is not reasonably practicable. In many circumstances treatment involving the simple addition of a chemical to the water supply, such as pH adjustment using lime, sodium hydroxide or other alkalis or phosphate dosing using orthophosphoric acid or one of the sodium orthophosphates, will be regarded as reasonably practicable. pH adjustment by passing water through a filter containing calcined dolomite or similar material may also be considered reasonably practicable. Other treatment such as alternating the supply of waters of different plumbo-solvency may also be practicable in some circumstances.

8.11 The causes of particulate lead in water supplies have not been fully elucidated. In some cases particulate lead may be caused by the quality of water put into supply, currently or in past years. Problems due to particulate lead should be reduced as water undertakers improve the aesthetic quality of water leaving treatment works and rehabilitate the mains in the distribution systems. A specific treatment to reduce particulate lead is not available at present.

*Lead pipe replacement*

8.12 In addition to the requirement in Regulation 24(1)(b), there are some situations where the water undertaker should consider replacing its part of lead service pipes. These could include the following –

(a) when the lead standard is breached at the time the water is made available to the consumer; and

(b) where the water undertaker has had to dig trenches to expose water mains or its part of the service pipes and it would be reasonably practicable to replace any lead service pipes, even though the water is already being treated to minimise the risk of exceeding the standard.

*Action when standard exceeded*

8.13 The occupier and the local authority environmental health officer (EHO) should be informed if a random daytime sample (see paragraph 2.5) from a property has exceeded the standard for lead. Advice should be given to draw off water which has been stationary in pipework before drawing water for drinking or cooking (Lead in Potable Water, Technical Note No2, DOE 1980). If the water undertaker is installing or planning to install treatment to reduce plumbo-solvency, then the occupier should be advised

44

that a reduction in the concentration of lead would be expected when this treatment has been introduced. If the water undertaker is already carrying out all reasonably practicable treatment to reduce plumbo-solvency or treatment is not planned because the risk relates to an insignificant part of the zone, the occupier should be informed of this situation. Occupiers should be advised that if the lead pipes on their property leading to the drinking water tap are replaced, the water undertaker will replace its section of the lead service pipe if requested to do so (in accordance with Regulation 24(1)(b)).

8.14 If no lead plumbing is present in the property and the infringement of the lead standard is thought to be due to galvanic corrosion of lead solder in copper plumbing, no remedial treatment is at present possible. In the circumstances the occupier and EHO should be informed of the situation which may be expected to improve with time. The property should be sampled again a year later. If concentrations are still above 50 µg/l the householder and EHO should be informed that replacement of the lead soldered joints is advisable.

**Copper and zinc**

8.15 Water undertakers may assume that there is no risk of the standards for copper and zinc being exceeded unless there is evidence to the contrary. If routine random daytime samples from consumers' taps indicate failure to meet the standard for copper and zinc in a water supply zone the cause of any failure should be investigated. If any failure is not related to the particular circumstances of the property, and failures occur elsewhere in the zone, water undertakers should consider what action could be taken to ensure compliance. An appropriate undertaking under Section 20(5)(b) should then be submitted. The occupier (and the EHO) should be informed if a random daytime sample from a property has exceeded the standard for copper or zinc.

# 9 Interpretation of Deterioration in Quality

9.1 Section 52(1)(b) of the Act places a duty on water undertakers, so far as is reasonably practicable, to ensure that there is, in general, no deterioration in the quality of water which is supplied.

9.2 Water quality changes are occurring all the time and many of these are seasonal or caused by meteorological events or operational processes such as blending, substitution of a groundwater source with a surface water derived supply or the provision of a standby supply. Also, a change in concentration of any substance which does not breach a prescribed maximum or minimum concentration does not in itself necessarily indicate a material deterioration in quality. The Secretaries of State will have regard to these factors in considering any notification of deterioration.

# 10 Applications for Relaxation
(Regulation 4)

10.1 Applications for relaxation under Regulation 4 should contain the following information:

(a) the relevant water supply zones (with a map if not already provided);

(b) the population supplied;

(c) the terms of the relaxation requested;

(d) relevant water quality data for the last three years;

(e) the cause of the infringement;

(f) the steps (if relevant) proposed to comply with the standard and their timescale;

(g) confirmation that the relevant local authorities have been informed under Regulation 4(3), and the names of those authorities; and

(h) any other information relevant to the application.

# 11 Provision of Information
(Regulation 30)

11.1 Water undertakers are required by Regulation 30(1) to make available to the public the record of water quality information they must maintain under Regulation 29. This record must be available for inspection at all reasonable hours and free of charge at those of their offices which are normally open to the public.

11.2 The intention of this provision is to enable consumers to inspect the record during normal working hours at offices which are within reasonable travelling distance. Water undertakers should keep the appropriate Department informed of the names and addresses of the offices where the record is available for public inspection.

11.3 Water undertakers are required by Regulation 30(4) to provide local authorities with information about the quality of water in their areas at least once a year. This is a minimum requirement. Many water undertakers currently have arrangements with local authorities under which they supply the local authorities with more frequent reports on the quality of water in their areas. Mutually acceptable arrangements of this nature are strongly recommended. Attention is also drawn to the powers available to local authorities under Section 59 of the Act to obtain information on water quality.

# ANNEX 1   Guidance Letters

The following guidance letters issued by the Department of the Environment and the Welsh Office to water undertakers contain information which is relevant to the provision of wholesome water. A copy of these letters is attached.

| | | |
|---|---|---|
| WP/1/1986 | Asbestos and drinking water | 20/2/86 |
| WP/12/1986 | Chlorination byproducts in drinking water | 4/9/86 |
| WP/4/1987 | Guidance for dealing with incidents and emergencies involving the release of radioactivity to the environment | 11/5/87 |
| WP/9/1987 | Water fluoridation schemes | 12/11/87 |
| WP/7/1988 | Coal tar pitch particles and polycylic aromatic hydrocarbons in drinking water | 1/11/88 |
| WP/2/1989 | Products based on polyacrylamide and acrylamide/acrylate copolymers | 10/2/89 |
| WP/3/1989 | Aluminium in drinking water | 13/2/89 |
| WP/5/1989 | Epoxy resin lining of water mains | 22/3/89 |
| WP/6/1989 | Cryptosporidium in water supplies | 22/3/89 |
| WP/15/1989 | Cryptosporidium in water supplies | 24/8/89 |
| WP/17/1989 | Lead in water | 29/9/89 |
| WP/18/1989 | Pesticides in drinking water | 29/9/89 |

DOE/Welsh Office


WP 1/1986                                                          20 February 1986


DOE Reference: WS/602/78
Welsh Office Ref: WEP/1274/1


To:    Chief Executives of Water Authorities
       in England and Wales


Dear Sir,


ASBESTOS AND DRINKING WATER


1.    Medical advice has been sought on possible health risks from asbestos in drinking
water. The DHSS Committee on Medical Aspects of the Contamination of Air, Soil and
Water has now provided the following statement which will be of interest to water
undertakers.

STATEMENT ON ASBESTOS AND DRINKING WATER

The Committee was asked to advise on the implication to the public health of the
concentrations and forms of asbestos found in a recent survey* of selected drinking
waters in the United Kingdom, particularly in relation to the use of asbestos cement
pipes in drinking water distribution systems. The only potential risk from the
presence of asbestos in drinking water which has been suggested as at all plausible,
is that of certain forms of cancer. The Committee has considered the substantial
body of research findings relevant to this question; it has found no convincing
evidence which indicates that the concentrations and forms of asbestos in drinking
water in the UK, including those derived from the use of asbestos cement pipes
according to current practice, represent a hazard to the health of the consumer. The
information assessed by this Committee suggests that, if there is any carcinogenic
risk to the consumer from exposure to asbestos in drinking water, it is of an
extremely low order and is not detectable by the methods currently available.

2.    A copy of this letter is being sent to the Water Companies' Association for
distribution to their members. We are also sending a copy to the Secretary of the Water
Authorities' Association; the Chief Engineer, Civil Engineering and Water Services
Directorate, Scottish Development Department; the Assistant Secretary, Water Service
Division, Department of the Environment for Northern Ireland and the heads of the Land
Drainage and Fisheries Divisions of MAFF.

3.    Enquiries on this letter should be directed in England to Mr O D Hydes (01-212
6359) Water Technical Division, Romney House, 43 Marsham Street, London SW1P 3PY
and in Wales to Mr J E Saunders (0222 823178) Water and Environmental Protection
Division, Welsh Office, Cathays Park, Cardiff CF1 8NQ.

50

4.    Finally, you will have noticed that this letter has been given a WP index number. This stands for Water Policy and is intended as a more accurate title than the former Water Information. In all other respects WP letters are identical with, and henceforth supersede, WI letters.

Yours faithfully


M G HEALEY                                L E TAYLOR
Water Technical Division                  Water and Environmental Protection Division
Department of the Environment             Welsh Office


* Conway, D M & Lacey, R F 'Asbestos in Drinking Water'
  Technical Report TR 202, Water Research Centre, Medmenham, March 1984.

DOE/Welsh Office

WP    12/1986                                                4 September 1986

DOE Reference: WS/1035/7
Welsh Office Reference; WEP/93/139/1

To:    Chief Executives of Water Authorities and Secretaries of Water Companies in
England and Wales

Dear Sir,

CHLORINATION BYPRODUCTS IN DRINKING WATER

1.    Medical advice has been sought on the possible health risks from chlorination
byproducts in drinking water. Over the past 18 months the DHSS Committee on Medical
Aspects of Air, Soil and Water has considered the relevant data from the areas of
epidemiology, animal carcinogenicity and mutagenicity.

2.    The Committe has now provided the attached statement which will be of interest to
water undertakers. The Committee's conclusions are restated below:

'We have found no sound reason to conclude that the consumption of the
byproducts of chlorination, in drinking-water which has been treated and
chlorinated according to current practices, increases the risk of cancer in humans.

The effective disinfection of water supplies is clearly of great importance in
maintaining public health. In our opinion, modification of chlorination processes
which have proved effective over many years, or the replacement of chlorination by
other disinfectants, is not required by the available data on cancer epidemiology,
animal carcinogenicity, and mutagenicity in relation to chlorination byproducts in
drinking water.'

3.    The Committee has also made recommendations for further research associated
with mutagenicity assays of concentrated extracts of chlorinated water and these are being
explored by the Water Research Centre. It has advised that further research using
epidemiological studies and long-term carcinogenicity bioassays is not appropriate at
present.

4.    When formulating their recommendations the Committee addressed the health risks
from chlorination byproducts in drinking water. It was not within their remit to consider
methods of water treatment designed to minimise the chlorination byproducts passing into
supply, the advantages these methods might offer and their costs. Some water undertakers
seeking to improve the aesthetic quality of the water they supply, to reduce growth of
organisms or increase the persistence of disinfectant residual within their distribution
systems, are now investigating such methods of treatment. The Department and the Welsh
Office are fully in favour of these investigations. They also wish strongly to endorse the
view of the Committee that effective disinfection of water supplies is of great importance
in maintaining public health.

5.    Enquiries on this letter should be directed in England to Mr O D Hydes (01-212 6359), Water Technical Division, Romney House, 43 Marsham Street, London SW1P 3PY and in Wales to Mr J E Saunders (0222 823178), Water and Environmental Protection Division, Welsh Office, Cathays Park, Cardiff CF1 3NQ.

6.    Copies of this letter and the statement are being sent to the Secretaries of the Water Authorities' Association, and the Water Companies Association; the Chief Engineer, Civil Engineering and Water Services Directorate, Scottish Development Department; the Assistant Secretary, Water Service Division, Department of the Environment for Northern Ireland, the heads of the Land Drainage and Fisheries Divisions of MAFF, and to the Chief Executive, Water Research Centre.

Yours faithfully

M G HEALEY
Water Technical Division
Department of the Environment

L E TAYLOR
Water and Environmental Protection Division
Welsh Office

DEPARTMENT OF HEALTH AND SOCIAL SECURITY

COMMITTEE ON MEDICAL ASPECTS OF THE CONTAMINATION OF AIR, SOIL
AND WATER CHLORINATION BYPRODUCTS

BACKGROUND

1.　　The disinfection of water by chlorination incidentally involves the reaction of
chlorine with organic substances, many of natural origin, which are typically present in
source waters. The chemicals which are formed as a result are referred to here as
'chlorination byproducts'; some, such as the trihalomethanes, are well characterised, but
there are many others that have still to be identified. The concentration of individual
chlorination byproducts found in drinking water varies but is typically of the order of a
few parts per thousand million (i.e. micrograms per litre).

2.　　Some of the individual byproducts of chlorination cause cancers in laboratory
animals when administered in large doses over long periods. It is therefore pertinent to
ask whether the regular consumption of chlorinated drinking water could increase the risk
of cancer in humans by virtue of its content of chlorination byproducts. We have
considered the relevant data from the areas of epidemiology, animal carcinogenicity and
mutagenicity.

EPIDEMIOLOGY

3.　　A large number of epidemiological studies has been undertaken, mainly in the
United States. Most of the studies were based on comparisons of cancer mortality or
incidence rates in the populations of contrasted areas where exposure to chlorination
byproducts was likely to differ as a consequence of differences in the chemical composition
of the source water, or in methods of water treatment, or both. Such geographical
comparisons could not adequately take into account differences in socioeconomic status,
occupation and personal habits (such as smoking, or diet), all of which have an important
effect on the risk of development of cancer; they were therefore more useful for
generating than testing hypotheses.

4.　　Although some of the geographical comparisons suggested possible associations
between cancers of various organs and the chlorination of drinking water, there was little
consistency between the results of the different studies. The most frequent associations
were with cancers of the bladder, colon and rectum and these cancers were therefore the
most promising for more detailed study.

5.　　There has been one series of geographical comparisons within the United Kingdom
with some relevance[1,2]. In common with many of the studies from the United States,
however, the measure of exposure was primarily intended to indicate the degree of
contamination of water sources prior to treatment: since the organic compounds present in
source waters include the precursors of chorination byproducts, the measure of exposure
may provide some indication of the concentration of chlorination byproducts in the treated
water supply. These studies found no consistent association between the measure of
exposure used and the incidence or mortality for any of the sites of cancer investigated,
which included cancers of the bladder, colon and rectum.

6.　　In contrast to geographical comparisons, studies of the case-control type are able to
incorporate estimates of individual exposure to chlorination byproducts, and information
on some of the other relevant factors such as socioeconomic status, occupation, smoking
and diet. More than a dozen such studies have been undertaken but none in the United
Kingdom. Although some have found associations between water chlorination and cancers
of various organs, including the bladder, colon, and rectum, none of the associations is

54

present consistently. In particular, the more recent studies, using detailed information from interviews rather than the sparser and probably less accurate data on death certificates, do not confirm the associations suggested by some of the earlier studies.

7. The epidemiological studies do not therefore demonstrate an effect on the risk of cancer to the consumer from chlorination byproducts in drinking water. The uncertainty inherent in the methods at present available for estimating exposures to chlorination byproducts, and the difficulty of interpreting small differences in cancer rates between populations against the usual background variability of such rates, means that risk cannot be totally excluded but also that further epidemiological studies are not likely to lead to substantial clarification.

## CARCINOGENICITY IN ANIMALS

8. Concentrated organic extracts from chlorinated drinking water have been used in several carcinogenicity studies. Such extracts contain many, but not all, of the organic compounds in the water from which they are derived, their composition depending on the method of extraction.

9. In one of the carcinogenicity studies[3], in which groups of rats and mice were given oral doses of concentrated organic extracts from chlorinated drinking water equivalent to at least 100 times the estimated daily intake of drinking water by humans, a dose-related increase in cancers was noted in rats, and a high incidence without a dose response in mice. This study was deficient in several respects, including the lack of suitable control groups of animals, and insufficient details of the pathological findings; cancers of the bladder, colon, or rectum were apparently not increased. None of the other studies, whether using oral administration (e.g. reference 4), subcutaneous injection or cutaneous application of extracts has been shown to cause cancer in the animals exposed.

10. Each of these studies had limitations, and none was an adequate test of the carcinogenicity of the extracts. However, the preparation of sufficient extract to permit a conventional carcinogenicity bioassay of adequate size and duration would be a major undertaking, and the interpretation of the results would be fraught with difficulty in view of the complex and variable composition of the concentrates. We do not therefore, recommend further long term carcinogenicity test of such extracts on whole animals at the present time.

## MUTAGENICITY

11. The results of mutagenicity tests on a substance are frequently used as an indication of its potential carcinogenicity. Much work has been done using concentrated extracts of chlorinated water in mutagenicity tests. As with the extracts used in the carcinogenicity studies, the composition depends on the method of extraction.

12. Concentrated organic extracts of chlorinated drinking water are strongly mutagenic in bacterial assays and *in vitro* tests using mammalian cells, but did not produce chromosome damage in mouse bone marrow in an *in vivo* study. The mutagenicity of the extracts in bacterial tests is typically reduced by the addition of liver microsomal enzymes, and the ability to produce structural chromosome aberrations in cultured mammalian cells is reduced in the presence of blood serum. We therefore consider it unlikely that chlorination byproducts in drinking water would be mutagenic in man following absorption from the gut and transport in the blood to the rest of the body via the liver. This deduction is consistent with the results of the *in vivo* tests.

13. There remains the theoretical possibility that a direct mutagenic action of chlorination byproducts on the mucosa lining the alimentary tract may lead to cancer. Insofar as the possible associations suggested by the initial epidemiological studies included associations with cancers of the colon and rectum (as noted in paragraph 4) this hypothesis merits further investigation.

55

## RECOMMENDATIONS FOR FURTHER RESEARCH

14.    We recommend that the results of the mutagenicity assays of concentrated extracts of chlorinated water should be explored further, by:
    (a)    chemical identification of the component(s) which are mutagenic *in vitro*:
    (b)    elucidation of the mechansms whereby metabolic activation systems, and blood serum, reduce the *in vitro* mutagenicity;
    (c)    investigation of the possible morphological effects, on the alimentary tract in experimental mammals, of short-term oral administration of concentrated extracts which are mutagenic *in vitro*.

15.    We advise that the following lines of research are not justified at present:
    (a)    epidemiological studies whose prinicipal purpose is to investigate human cancer rates in relation to indirect measures of exposure to chlorination byproducts. Such exposure data, however, may be incorporated usefully in the analysis of other studies of cancer epidemiology;
    (b)    long term carcinogenicity bioassays of concentrated extracts of chlorinated water.

## CONCLUSIONS

16.    We have found no sound reason to conclude that the consumption of the by-products of chlorination, in drinking water which has been treated and chlorinated according to current practices, increases the risk of cancer in humans.

17.    The effective disinfection of water supplies is clearly of great importance in maintaining public health. In our opinion, modification of chlorination processes which have proved effective over many years, or the replacement of chlorination by other disinfectants, is not required by the available data on cancer epidemiology, animal carcinogenicity, and mutagenicity in relation to chlorination byproducts in drinking water.

## REFERENCES

1.    Beresford, S. A. A.: The relationship between water quality and health in the London area. Int. J. Epidem. 1981; *10*: 103-115.

2.    Beresford, S. A. A.: Cancer incidence and reuse of drinking water Am. J. Epidemiol. 1983; *117*: 258-68.

3.    Truhaut, R., Gak, J. C., Graillot, C: Recherches sur les risques pouvant resulter de la pollution chimique des eaux d'alimentation – I. Water Research 1979: *13*: 689-97.

4.    Kool, H. J., Kuper, F., van Haerigen, H., Koeman, J. H.: A carcinogenicity study with mutagenic organic concentrates of drinking water in the Netherlands. Fed. Chem. Toxic. 1985; *23*: 79-85.

August 1986

DOE/Welsh Office
WP 4/1987

DOE Reference: WS/1053/4
Welsh Office Reference: WEP 104/57/1                                11 May 1987

To:    Chief Executives of Water Authorities and Secretaries of Water Companies in
       England and Wales

Dear Sir,

GUIDANCE FOR DEALING WITH INCIDENTS AND EMERGENCIES
INVOLVING THE RELEASE OF RADIOACTIVITY TO THE ENVIRONMENT

Following the accident at Chernobyl, the Government instigated a review of the
arrangements for dealing with nuclear emergencies that might affect the UK. This resulted
in a report to Ministers and in response to a Parliamentary Question the Prime Minister
on 18 December 1986 made a statement, the text of which is annexed to this letter.

These developments prompted the issue of new Guidance as above and we now enclose a
copy which supersedes the 'Instructions in the Event of an Accidental Release of
Radioactivity' dated December 1983. If you wish to see a copy contact Mr White, Room
B454, ext 5486.

Except for Appendix 3 listing establishments for which emergency folders have been
prepared, all appendices have been removed from your copy of the Guidance because they
concern only Government departments. You will see that the possible contamination of
public water supplies by radioactive substances features prominently in the Guidance and
we draw your attention particularly to the contents of section 9 (General Advice to Water
Authorities) and to section 10 concerning sampling.

Paragraph 10.21 states that a supplement dealing specifically with sampling procedures will
be issued shortly. This is currently being prepared by the working group established jointly
by the Department, the Water Authorities Association and the Water Companies
Association. We expect it to be available in the autumn. The working group is also
examining all aspects of existing contingency arrangements and will recommend any
necessary improvements. Apart from this, the Guidance will be reviewed regularly by the
Department and amendments issued as necessary.

Enquiries on this letter should be directed in England to Mr P D Bell (01-212 5589),
Water Technical Division, Romney House, 43 Marsham Street, London SW1P 3PY, and
in Wales to Mr J Atkins (0222 823235), Water and Environmental Protection Division,
Welsh Office, Cathays Park, Cardiff CF1 3NQ.

Copies of this letter and the enclosures are being sent to the Secretaries of the Water
Authorities Association and the Water Companies Association; the Chief Engineer, Civil
Engineering and Water Services Directorate, Scottish Development Department; the
Assistant Secretary, Water Services Division, Department of the Environment Northern
Ireland and the Heads of the Land Drainage and Fisheries Divisions of MAFF.

Yours faithfully

M G HEALEY                             L E TAYLOR
Water Technical Division               Water and Environmental Protection Division
Department of the Environment          Welsh Office

STATEMENT MADE BY THE PRIME MINISTER TO PARLIAMENT ON
18 DECEMBER 1986

'The first stage of a thorough review of existing emergency plans and procedures in the light of experience of the Chernobyl accident has now been completed by the Cabinet Office in consultation with the appropriate Government Departments and agencies concerned.

The existing plans are addressed specifically to an accident occurring within the United Kingdom and cover both the emergency procedures at the site and offsite arrangements to protect the public. They continue to provide a valid basis for the response to any nuclear accident in the United Kingdom. However, the Government have decided that planning needs to provide more specifically for the response to a nuclear accident outside the United Kingdom.

Detailed planning is now in hand. Among other things this will need to ensure nationwide monitoring coverage and, in the light of expert assessment of the results of monitoring, for the dissemination of appropriate advice and information to the general public. In the event of any future nuclear accident overseas affecting the United Kingdom the Secretary of State for the Environment will take the lead in co-ordinating Government action.

At the same time, the Government will continue to work with our international partners both in the International Atomic Energy Agency and elsewhere to improve the arrangements for co-ordinated international action. In the meantime, the two recently signed International Atomic Energy Agency sponsored conventions should ensure earlier and more effective notification and dissemination of information than occurred in the case of the Chernobyl accident.

I shall make a further statement when the detailed planning now in hand has been completed and appropriate steps will be taken to make the new arrangements known to the public and to all the authorities concerned'.


MGH3004 1

DOE/WP 9/1987

DOE Reference: WS/34/2/2

12 November 1987

To: Chief Executives of Water Authorities and
    Water Companies in England

Dear Sir,

## WATER FLUORIDATION SCHEMES

This letter gives guidance on the role of water undertakers in fluoridation schemes, and should be read together with the letter of 15 November 1985 which gives advice on the provisions of the Water (Fluoridation) Act 1985.

Four documents are being sent under cover of this letter. They are:

a.    a Code of Practice on Technical Aspects of Fluoridation of Water Supplies;

b.    a Model Agreement as a basis for discussions between health authorities and water undertakers on the terms under which fluoridation is carried out;

c.    the terms of the indemnity which the Secretary of State for Social Services is providing for water undertakers operating fluoridation schemes;

and
d.    a circular issued by DHSS to health authorities on fluoridation.

## THE ROLE OF WATER UNDERTAKERS

The Department expects water undertakers to be chiefly concerned with the technical feasibility rather than the principle of fluoridation which is a matter for health authorities to consider. To this end it would be helpful if undertakers made available to regional and district health authorities on request an assessment of the technical feasibility and estimated costs of fluoridation to assist health authorities in deciding whether to make formal applications for a scheme. In determining technical feasibility, undertakers will need to take fully into account any long term proposals or possibilities for transferring water from one area to another, and the statutory limitations on providing fluoridated water outside the area covered by the possible scheme (section 1(6) of the Water (Fluoridation) Act 1985). This may involve explaining to the health authorities which areas it would be feasible to fluoridate without the scheme being endangered by future water supply strategy.

The cost of fluoridation schemes is borne by the health authorities concerned, and all costs incurred by water undertakers on schemes should therefore be recompensed.

In the interests of simplicity the water undertaker should normally deal with the regional health authority on matters affecting a scheme which covers or may cover more than one district health authority area, as the regional authority will be acting as a co-ordinator for the district authorities. Where the regional authority does not take this role, one district will be nominated to take on co-ordination for all the authorities involved.

## MODEL AGREEMENT

If the water undertaker agrees in principle to provide a fluoridation scheme in accordance with the application of one or more DHAs, it will need to negotiate the terms of an agreement so that the rights and obligations of each party are clearly understood and the full costs of fluoridation are borne by health authorities. The Model Agreement enclosed with this letter has been prepared by DHSS following discussions with representatives of the water industry and this Department. It sets out the principal items to be taken into account in reaching an agreement and forms a basis for discussion. Variations may be necessary in the light of local conditions or views.

## THE CODE OF PRACTICE

This Code updates and replaces guidance given in the Second Biennial Report of the Standing Technical Advisory Committee on Water Quality published in 1981. Water undertakers should comply with the provisions of this Code. In view of its comprehensive nature the Department will no longer be inspecting and approving fluoridation installations, or requiring information on their performance. Health authorities will make their own arrangements with undertakers about monitoring performance in order to comply with their obligations under section 1(5) of the 1985 Act. The Department will co-ordinate any future revisions of the Code.

## INDEMNITY AGAINST LEGAL ACTION

The Secretary of State for Social Services will continue to indemnify water undertakers carrying out fluoridation schemes requested by health authorities against legal challenge. The terms of the new indemnity are attached. As the Act provides clear power for water authorities to fluoridate, the indemnity no longer covers this point. It does however indemnify against the unlikely event of any damages awarded in respect of adverse effects on a person's health caused by fluoridation.

## DISTRIBUTION OF DOCUMENTS

Copies of this letter and the attached documents are being sent to the Water Companies' Association for distribution to their members and for information to the Secretary of the Water Authorities Association; the Chief Engineer, Civil Engineering and Water Services Directorates, Scottish Development Department; the head of the Water and Environmental Protection Division, Welsh Office, the Assistant Secretary, Conservation Division, Department of the Environment for Northern Ireland; the heads of the Land Drainage and Fisheries Divisions of Maff, and the head of the Family Practitioner Services Division 2A(1) of DHSS.

## ENQUIRIES

Enquiries about this letter, the Model Agreement, and the indemnity may be addressed to C P Douglas, DOE, Room A444, Romney House, 43 Marsham Street, London, SW1P 3PY (01-212 6355) and enquiries about the Code of Practice may be addressed to O D Hydes at the same address (01-212 6359).

Yours faithfully


M G HEALEY
Head of Water Technical Division
Department of the Environment

DOE Reference: WS/34/8/1
Welsh Office Reference: WEP/123/19/1


To:  Chief Executives of Water Authorities and Secretaries
     of Water Companies in England and Wales



Dear Sir


COAL TAR PITCH PARTICLES AND POLYCYCLIC AROMATIC
HYDROCARBONS IN DRINKING WATER


INTRODUCTION

1.     An advisory limit of 0.2 microgram per litre for the total concentration of six
specified polycyclic aromatic hydrocarbons (PAH) was proposed by the World Health
Organisation (WHO) in the 1970 European Standards for Drinking Water. In 1980, this
limit was incorporated as a standard in the EC Directive relating to the Quality of Water
intended for Human Consumption (80/778/EEC) and the standard has been mandatory in
the UK since July 1985. It now relates to individual samples following the advice on
interpretation of EC Directive standards given in Water Policy Letter WP1/1988 issued on
10 March 1988. A guideline value of 0.01 microgram per litre for benzo [a] pyrene, an
individual PAH, was recommended by WHO in the Guidelines for Drinking Water
Quality published in 1984.

2.     Advice has been sought from the Department of Health Committee on the Medical
Aspects of the Contamination of Air, Soil and Water (CASW) on the possible health risks
from coal tar pitch particles (CTPP) and PAH in drinking water. This letter outlines the
background to the problem, sets out the medical advice received and gives interim
guidance on the monitoring for PAH in drinking water.

BACKGROUND

3.     From the last century to the mid 1970s most water distribution mains made of cast
or ductile iron were given an internal anti-corrosion coating of coal tar pitch before being
laid in the ground. Coal tar pitch can contain up to 50% of PAH and water supplied
through mains lined with coal tar pich has been found occasionally to contain PAH in
solution and in suspension. That in solution arises mainly through leaching from the
coating while that in suspension comes from the shedding of particles as a result of
deterioration of the coating. Some PAH are known to be carcinogenic in animals and may
be carcinogenic in humans. It should be noted that some mains are lined with bitumen
which is exclusively of petroleum or asphalt origin and normally contains very low levels of
PAH.

4.     A major survey for PAH in water was carried out for the Department of the
Environment (DOE) in the mid 1970s by the Water Research Centre (WRc) and was

reported in TR 158 published in 1981[1]. It was found that PAH concentrations in groundwater sources were extremely low and that any PAH present in surface water sources was removed by coagulation, sedimentation and filtration at treatment works. Most drinking water at consumers' taps contained PAH concentrations well below 0.2 microgram per litre. A few samples exceeded this concentration and it was shown that the PAH consisted almost entirely of fluorathene, a PAH which is not considered to be carcinogenic, derived from the coal tar pitch lining. Since 1977 water undertakers have ceased laying mains coated with coal tar pitch following a recommendation stemming from that survey. The report also recommended further study of the occurrence of CTPP in drinking water and an assessment of the public health significance of CTPP and PAH in drinking water.

5.    In the early 1980s, WRc carried out an investigation for DOE on the occurrence of CTPP in drinking water. This work has now been published[2]. It showed that sediments in water mains occasionally contain substantial quantities of CTPP and consequently of PAH and concluded that situations which disturb mains linings and sediments, such as mains renovations may release CTPP into drinking water. The work also showed that the techniques for direct quantification of CTPP in drinking water are extremely complex and unsuitable for routine monitoring.

MEDICAL ADVICE

6.    In view of these findings CASW was asked to advise upon appropriate standards for PAH in drinking water, particularly with regard to CTPP and whether further research on the biological significance of CTPP to the consumer would be feasible. The full advice received is appended to this letter.

7.    In summary CASW have endorsed the mandatory standard of 0.2 microgram per litre for the total concentration of the six specified PAH and the WHO guideline of 0.01 microgram per litre for benzo [a] pyrene. It was considered unlikely that further research would determine readily the relative biological significance of particulate and soluble PAH.

NEXT STEPS

8.    The Department considers that all water undertakers should carry out surveys for PAH in drinking water beyond present monitoring requirements to determine whether these values are being approached or exceeded within their distribution systems. Consultations are now proceeding with the Water Authorities Association, Water Companies' Association and the Water Research Centre on the method of survey with a view to issuing further advice very shortly. The information generated by these surveys should enable water undertakers to develop remedial programmes should these prove necessary.

USE OF CHLORINE DIOXIDE

9.    There is evidence that the use of chlorine dioxide as a disinfectant and for taste and odour control can give rise to substantially elevated PAH concentrations in samples of water from consumers' taps compared with those obtained when chlorine gas is used.

---

[1]Technical Report TR158. A survey of Polycyclic Aromatic Hydrocarbon levels in British Waters, Water Research Centre, January 1981.

[2]Report PRD 1778–M. Coal-Tar Pitch Particles in Drinking Water, WRc Environment, May 1988.

Therefore water undertakers are advised to monitor carefully at consumers' taps any supplies treated with chlorine dioxide which are distributed through mains lined with coal tar pitch. If concentrations greater than 0.2 microgram per litre for the six specified PAH or 0.01 microgram per litre for benzo [a] pyrene are confirmed, the use of chlorine dioxide should be discontinued.

ENQUIRIES

10.    Enquiries on this letter should be directed in England to Mr O D Hydes (01-276 8213) Water Technical Division, Romney House, 43 Marsham Street, London SW1P 3PY and in Wales to Mr J E Saunders (0222 823178) Water and Environmental Protection Division, Welsh Office, Cathays Park, Cardiff CF1 3NQ.

11.    Copies of this letter and the appendix are being sent to the Secretaries of the Water Authorities Association and the Water Companies' Association; the Chief Engineer, Civil Engineering and Water Services Directorate, Scottish Development Department; the Assistant Secretary, Water Service Division, Department of the Environment for Northern Ireland; the Heads of the Land Drainage and Fisheries Divisions of MAFF and the Chief Executive of the Water Research Centre.


Yours faithfully



M G HEALEY                              A H H JONES
Water Technical Division                Water and Environmental Protection Division
Department of the Environment           Welsh Office

COMMITTEE ON THE MEDICAL ASPECTS OF THE CONTAMINATION OF AIR, SOIL AND WATER

COAL TAR PITCH PARTICLES AND POLYCYCLIC AROMATIC HYDROCARBONS IN DRINKING WATER

a.    The Committee notes the maximum admissible concentration of 0.2 microgram per litre for the sum of six specified polycyclic aromatic hydrocarbons (PAH), set by the European Communities Directive relating to the Quality of Water intended for Human Consumption (80/778/EEC, parameter 56) and considers adherence to this limit to be a practical way to avoid undue exposure to PAH through drinking water.

b.    The Committee endorses the World Health Organisation guideline of not more than 0.01 microgram per litre for benzo [a] pyrene in drinking water.

c.    PAH may be present in drinking water in soluble or particulate form. Particles from coal tar pitch linings in the distribution network can increase very substantially the concentration of PAH in the tap water. The Committee notes that approximately 75% by length of the mains laid for the water undertakers are of ductile or cast iron, and the majority of these have been coated internally with coal tar pitch; the proportion is decreasing as coal tar pitch has not been used for this purpose since the late 1970s and such pipes are gradually being re-lined or replaced.

d.    There is no information which indicates convincingly that PAH in coal tar pitch particles or other particulate form is of either greater or lesser biological significance to the consumer that PAH dissolved in the drinking water. Since it is unlikely that the issue could be resolved readily by available research methods, it is advisable to regard both soluble and particulate PAH as having equal biological significance.

e.    Analysis for PAH in drinking water should use methods which extract both soluble and particulate PAH as completely as possible. The presence of visible particles of coal tar pitch in tap water is clearly undesirable.

May 1988

DOE/WELSH OFFICE
WP/2/1989


DOE Reference: WS/34/1/47
WELSH OFFICE Reference: WEP/93/8/1


To Chief Executives of Water Authorities
and Secretaries of Water Companies
in England and Wales                                          10 February 1989



Dear Sir


COMMITTEE ON CHEMICALS AND MATERIALS OF CONSTRUCTION FOR USE
IN PUBLIC WATER SUPPLY AND SWIMMING POOLS


PRODUCTS BASED ON POLYACRYLAMIDE AND ACRYLAMIDE/ACRYLATE
COPOLYMERS


1.    Products based on polyacrylamide (made by polymerising acrylamide monomer)
and acrylamide/acrylate copolymers (made by polymerising acrylamide monomer and an
acrylate based monomer) were first approved by the Committee in the late 1960s as being
unobjectionable on health grounds for use as coagulant aids in the treatment of water for
public supply. All these products are referred to below as polyacrylamides. The approvals
are currently subject to the following conditions –

    (i)    No batch must contain more than 0.05% of free acrylamide monomer based
    on the active polymer content.

    (ii)    The dose used must average no more than 0.5 mg/l and never exceed 1.0
    mg/l of the active polymer.

    (iii)    An upper limit for the content of free acrylamide monomer must be stated
    by the supplier for every batch.

    (iv)    The method to be used for the analysis for free acrylamide monomer in the
    polymer is that published in the series Methods for the Examination of Waters and
    Associated Materials entitled 'Determination of Acrylamide Monomer in Waters
    and Polymers 1987' (HMSO, 1988, ISBN 011 752039)

Note: 'active polymer content' means the amount of polyacrylamide in the product.

2.    These approvals were granted following consideration of published toxicological
data for polyacrylamides containing various concentrations of acrylamide monomer (DD
McCollister et al, Toxicology and Applied Pharmacology 1964,6,172). In recent years
much more information about the toxicology of acrylamide has become available. The
Committee has therefore sought advice from the Department of Health Committee on the
Medical Aspects of the Contamination of Air, Soil and Water (CASW) and has reviewed
the conditions of approval for the use of polyacrylamides in the treatment of water for
public supply.

3.    Studies have shown that acrylamide monomer is mutagenic in cells in culture, and in mammalian somatic and germ cells *in vivo*. There is limited evidence, from one study, that acrylamide monomer can produce cancers in the rat, although the validity of this study has been disputed, and the research is being repeated. In mice, acrylamide monomer can initiate skin tumours.

4.    The approved use of polyacrylamides, subject to the current conditions, could lead to a maximum theoretical concentration of 0.5 μg/l of acrylamide in drinking water. This concentration would result in exposures which are much lower than those associated with an increased risk of cancer in animals. It is not known what, if any, concentration of acrylamide in drinking water occurs as a consequence of the approved use of polyacrylamides, since analytical techniques to measure concentrations of 0.5 μg/l or less of acrylamide in water are not available. In particular it is not known whether acrylamide at such a low concentration remains unaltered by the subsequent stages of water treatment, notably chlorination. Research commissioned by the Department of the Environment is in progress to develop appropriate analytical methods and to investigate the reaction, if any, between acrylamide and chlorine.

5.    There is no direct evidence that the current use of polyacrylamides leads to the presence of acrylamide in drinking water, or to any risk to those who drink the water. However, as a precautionary measure, the Committee endorses the recommendation by CASW that the maximum content of acrylamide in polyacrylamides used as coagulant aids in the treatment of water for public supply should be reduced to its lowest practicable level.

6.    The Committee has decided to reduce from 0.050% to 0.025% the maximum permitted content of acrylamide monomer in these products. The Committee propose that this change should apply to all products supplied and used after 1 September 1989. This will allow existing stocks of these products, which contain between 0.025 and 0.050% of acrylamide, to be used up.

7.    The Committee has also decided that the average and maximum dose for water treatment should be reduced from 0.50 mg/l to 0.25 mg/l and 1.00 mg/l to 0.50 mg/l respectively. The Committee has agreed that this change should apply immediately.

8.    Thus polyacrylamides can continue to be used for the treatment of water for public supply provided the changed conditions set out in paragraphs 6 and 7 are met. These are that –

(i)    No batch must contain more than 0.025% of free acrylamide monomer based on the active polymer content.

(ii)    That dose used must average no more than 0.25 mg/l and never exceed 0.50 mg/l of the active polymer.

Manufacturers and suppliers of polyacrylamides have been advised of these changes to the condition of approval.

9.    The Committee will review the approval of these products again when the repeat carcinogenicity study referred to in paragraph 3 and the research studies mentioned in paragraph 4 are complete. The results of the research studies are not expected to be available for at least one year.

10.    Any queries on this letter should be directed to Mr O D Hydes, Room A439, Romney House, 43 Marsham Street, London SW1P 3PY, telephone 01 276 8213.

11.   Copies of this letter are being sent to the Secretaries of the Water Authorities Association and the Water Companies' Association; the Chief Engineer, Civil Engineering and Water Services Directorate, Scottish Development Department; the Assistant Secretary, Water Service Division, Department of the Environment for Northern Ireland; the Heads of the Land Drainage and Fisheries Divisions of MAFF and the Chief Executive of the Water Research Centre.


Yours faithfully



M G HEALEY                            A H H JONES
Drinking Water Division               Water and Environmental Protection Division
Department of the Environment         Welsh Office

DOE/WATER OFFICE
WP/3/1989


DOE Reference: WS/34/5/1
WELSH OFFICE Reference: WEP 32/12/2


To: Chief Executives of Water
    Authorities and Secretaries of
    Water Companies in England and Wales                    13 February 1989



Dear Sir,


## ALUMINIUM IN DRINKING WATER


1.    The purpose of this letter is to pass on to you medical advice on the use of
aluminium compounds in drinking water treatment.

## BACKGROUND

2.    Aluminium compounds have long been established in most parts of the world as
coagulants in water treatment. Approval of their use was given in the UK by the
Department's Committee on Chemical and Materials in 1976 when the Committee issued,
for the first time, a list of traditional or commonly used chemicals which were considered
to be unobjectionable on health grounds for the treatment of water for public supply.

3.    Medical advice on the possible health risks from aluminium in drinking water was
again sought in 1985 when the Department and Welsh Office were considering policy on
applications from water undertakers for derogations under Article 9 or delays under
Article 20 of the EC Drinking Water Directive (80/778/EEC) to supply water containing
average aluminium concentrations in excess of the Directive standard of 200 microgram of
aluminium per litre. Article 9 relates to natural aluminium and Article 20 to residual
aluminium from the use of aluminium compounds in water treatment.

4.    The Department of Health Committee on the Medical Aspects of the
Contamination of Air Soil and Water (CASW) considered the relevant data on aluminium
at that time and as a result of their advice the Department and Welsh Office included the
following paragraph in the decision letters on derogation and delay applications –

> "The Department's medical advisers have noted the hypothesis that aluminium may
> be a cause of Alzheimer's disease, a type of dementia. This hypothesis cannot be
> discounted completely, but neither has any connection been established. Research
> into this disease is continuing and it may become necessary in future years to
> reassess the advice. For this reason and because high aluminium concentrations in
> potable waters are aesthetically undesirable, Article 9 derogation applications have
> been granted but with a review period of five years. Article 20 delays have also
> been restricted to a maximum of five years ie until 1990".

5.    Subsequently the Department and Welsh Office has advised water undertakers that
all existing Article 9 derogations for parameters affecting the aesthetic quality of drinking
water, including aluminium, should be phased out by 1995.

## MEDICAL ADVICE

6.    Since 1985 CASW have kept under review the possible health risks from aluminium in drinking water. In November 1988, CASW considered papers based on some 200 references to studies on the possible relationship between aluminium and Alzheimer's disease, including the epidemiological study by Dr C N Martyn and his co-workers which was published subsequently in the Lancet on 14 January 1989. CASW concluded that:

(i)    it has not been established that a reduction in the aluminium intake of the general population would be likely to reduce the incidence of Alzheimer's disease;

(ii)    the association between Alzheimer's disease and aluminium concentrations in drinking-water, suggested by recent studies in Norway and the UK, was too tentative to justify changes in the use of aluminium sulphate in water treatment; and

(iii)    further research is important, particularly on the bioavailability of aluminium from all sources.

Note: conclusion (ii) covers other aluminium compounds which may be used in water treatment such as aluminium chloride, aluminium chlorohydrate and polyaluminium chloride.

7.    These conclusions, which have been endorsed by the Government's medical advisers, have been accepted by the Department and Welsh Office. There are therefore no grounds for amending the previous advice as summarised in paragraph 4 above.

8.    Research on the bioavailability of aluminium from food and water is commencing at the Trace Metabolism Unit at Southampton with funding from the Ministry of Agriculture Fisheries and Food. Further epidemiological and neuropathological research is in progress at the Medical Research Council units in Southampton and Newcastle. Research into Alzheimer's disease in general, and into the aluminium hypothesis in particular, is expanding nationally and internationally. This research will be kept under review by CASW.

## ACTION BY WATER UNDERTAKERS

9.    It follows from the medical advice that there is no need for water undertakers to change current good practices regarding the use of aluminium compounds in drinking water treatment. Water undertakers should continue with their programmes of remedial action to comply with the aluminium standard in the EC Directive and ensure that all Article 20 delay programmes are complete by 1990 and all existing Article 9 derogations are phased out by 1995 at the latest.

10.    Water undertakers are reminded of their agreement to inform those responsible for haemodialysis of patients in the National Health Service and in private practice when the concentration of aluminium in water supplies is likely to exceed 30 microgram per litre.

## ENQUIRES

11.    Any queries on this letter should be directed in England to Mr O D Hydes (Room A4.39, telephone 01-276 8213) and in Wales to Mr J E Saunders, Welsh Office, Cathays Park, Cadiff CF1 3NQ (telephone 0222-823178).

12.    Copies of this letter are being sent to the Secretaries of the Water Authorities Association and the Water Companies' Association; the Chief Engineer, Civil Engineering and Water Services Directorate, Scottish Development Department; the Assistant Secretary, Water Service Division, Department of the Environment for Northern Ireland; the Heads of the Land Drainage and Fisheries Divisions of MAFF and the Chief Executive of the Water Research Centre.

Yours faithfully

M G HEALEY
Drinking Water Division
Department of the Environment

A H H JONES
Water and Environmental Protection Division
Welsh Office

DOE REFERENCE: WS 34/1/32
WELSH OFFICE REFERENCE: WEP 74/63/1            22 March 1989

To: Chief Executives of Water Authorities and Secretaries of Water Companies in England and Wales

Dear Sir

EPOXY RESIN LINING OF WATER MAINS

1.    We refer to letters of 15 March 1985 and 11 July 1986 which indicated the position then on applications before the DOE Committee on Chemicals and Materials of Construction for use in Public Water Supply and Swimming Pools (CCM) relating to the use of epoxy resin formulations for the lining of water mains. These letters also gave interim advice on the use of these formulations.

2.    Reports on field tests to determine concentrations of leached chemicals and further toxicological tests on major components of one formulation have been reviewed recently by the Department of Health Committee on the Medical Aspects of the Contamination of Air Soil and Water (CASW). Their conclusions have been taken into account by the CCM which has now approved GEOPOX GX014 (manufactured by Mercol Descaling Company Ltd) as being unobjectionable on health grounds for use in the lining of water mains. The approval is subject to the following conditions –

    a.    All water undertakers and contractors should apply the linings in accordance with the In-situ Epoxy Resin Lining of Water Mains – Operational Guideline Manual incorporating a Code of Practice prepared by the Water Research Centre (Source Document for the Water Mains Rehabilitation Manual, 2nd Edition, Water Research Centre, 1989).

    b.    The resin should be manufactured under the effective control of a BS 5750 Quality System and approved by a third party certification organization (such as the British Standards Institution or the Water Industry Certification Scheme).

    c.    Lining equipment should be fitted with flow and mix ratio monitoring devices. As an interim measure, and only until 31 March 1990, contractors who in the recent past have been lining water mains with GEOPOX GX 014 may continue to use equipment not fitted with such devices provided that routine weight checks of the resin and hardener output from the delivery hoses are made to ensure that the mix ratio is within specification.

3.    We should be grateful if you could bring this letter to the attention of officers in your undertaking who are involved in lining activities. The letter will also be of interest to those involved in the preparation of programmes of work to achieve compliance with the standards in the EC 'Drinking Water' Directive. We expect that epoxy resin lining will be particularly valuable in situations where cement mortar lining would be likely to give rise to pH values in excess of the Directive standard for extended periods.

4.    Any queries on this letter should be directed to Mr O D Hydes, Room A439, Romney House, 43 Marsham Street, London SW1P 3PY, telephone 01-276 8213.

5.    Copies of this letter are being sent to the Secretaries of the Water Authorities Association and the Water Companies' Association; the Chief Engineer, Civil Engineering and Water Services Directorate, Scottish Development Department; the Assistant Secretary, Water Service Division, Department of the Environment for Northern Ireland; the Heads of the Land Drainage and Fisheries Divisions of MAFF and the Chief Executive of the Water Research Centre.


Yours faithfully



M G HEALEY                          A H H JONES
Drinking Water Division             Water and Environmental Protection Division
Department of Environment           Welsh Office

DOE/WELSH OFFICE
WP/6/1989


DOE Reference:           WS 34/15/5
Welsh Office Reference:   WEP 93/74/1


To: Chief Executives of Water Authorities and Secretaries of Water Companies in
    England and Wales


22 March 1989


Dear Sir


CRYPTOSPORIDIUM IN WATER SUPPLIES


1.    You will be aware from the press release issued by Thames Water on 25 February
1989 of the discovery of Cryptosporidium in water supplies in Swindon and Oxford and
intermittently in some other parts of their supply area. Before the press release was issued
the Department of the Environment informed the Water Authorities Association, the
Water Companies' Association and water undertakers, either by telephone or by message,
of the position. This letter provides further information and advice.

2.    At Annex A are the texts of answers given by Michael Howard to Parliamentary
Questions from Andrew Smith, Simon Coombs and Keith Raffan. These answers, *inter
alia*, contain a brief account of the experiences of Thames Water, comment upon the
public health significance of Cryptosporidium in water supplies and announce the decision
to set up a group of experts under the Chairmanship of Sir John Badenoch to advise upon
the subject. The terms of reference of the group are attached at Annex B.

3.    As the water industry has little experience of Cryptosporidium, we attach at Annex
C a note prepared by the Water Research Centre and checked by our Medical Advisers. It
provides background information upon the organism and the associated illness, refers to
outbreaks of the illness which have been associated one way or another with water,
discusses the effectiveness of water treatment processes and outlines plans for research.
We understand that Thames Water have circulated a note to water undertakers upon their
operational experiences. We trust that these two notes provide helpful backgrounds for the
industry.

4.    Advice on monitoring for micro-organisms, including pathogens, in water supplies is
given in Report 71, the Bacteriological Examination of Drinking Water Supplies.
Essentially, Report 71 states that the search for organisms (coliforms and faecal coliforms)
indicative of faecal pollution is universally accepted for the routine monitoring of drinking
water supplies and advises that the direct search for pathogenic organisms is not necessary
routinely. There are, however, occasions when investigation for faecal pathogens may be
necessary, for example, when a water supply is suspected of transmitting disease. This
advice has been followed by water undertakers for many years and is endorsed by the
Department and the Welsh Office.

73

5.   After consulting Medical Advisers, the Department and the Welsh Office believe that it is premature to modify the advice of Report 71 in the light of the limited information currently available about Cryptosporidium in water supplies and at present we are not proposing routine monitoring for Cryptosporidium in water supplies. In addition we do not at present recommend water undertakers to modify water treatment processes where routine tests show that the drinking water meets the standards for coliforms and faecal coliforms and there is no evidence to link the supply with outbreaks of illness.

6.   Sir John Badenoch's expert group will provide advice as soon as possible on these issues and, in particular, whether any measures are needed to deal with this problem on a long term basis.

7.   It is, of course, essential, as ever, for water undertakers to maintain a close liaison with Environmental Health Officers (EHO) and Medical Officers for Environmental Health (MOEH) within their areas and also with the Public Health Laboratory Service. If there is any evidence of a possible link between illness and water supply the water undertakers, in consultation with EHO and MOEH, should take appropriate action. This action may include monitoring for other organisms including Cryptosporidium, issuing advice to consumers, providing alternative water supplies and changes to operational procedures. We must stress the importance in such circumstances of keeping others, including Government Departments, fully informed.

8.   Any queries on this letter should be directed in England to Mr O D Hydes (Room A4.39, Telephone 01-276 8213), and in Wales to Mr J E Saunders, Welsh Office, Cathays Park, Cardiff CF1 3NQ (Telephone 0222 823178).

9.   Copies of this letter are being sent to the Secretaries of the Water Authorities Association and the Water Companies' Association; the Chief Medical Officer, Department of Health; the Director of Public Health Laboratory Service; the Chief Engineer, Civil Engineering and Water Services Directorate, Scottish Development Department; the Assistant Secretary, Water Services Division Department of the Environment for Northern Ireland; the Heads of the Land Drainage, Fisheries and Food Safety Divisions of MAFF; and the Chief Executive of the Water Research Centre. The information and background of this letter is also being sent to the local authority associations.

Yours faithfully

M G HEALEY
Drinking Water Division
Department of the Environment

A H H JONES
Water and Environmental Protection Division
Welsh Office

28 February 1989

CRYPTOSPORIDIA

Mr. Andrew Smith: To ask the Secretary of State for the Environment what action he is taking to tackle the outbreak of cryptosporidia contamination in the Thames water authority's Farmoor reservoir: if he will initiate a full inquiry into the causes of this outbreak: what action will be taken to prevent a recurrence of this outbreak; how far the levels of cryptosporidia contamination exceeded normal safety standards; and when this contamination was first discovered.

Mr. Howard: A possible link between a diarrhoel illness called cryptosporidiosis in the Oxford and Swindon areas and the water supply from Thames water authority's Farmoor treatment works was first identified a little over a week ago.

On finding cryptosporidia organisms in the treatment works and the distribution system on 20 February, Thames Water, in conjunction with local health authorities, immediately advised the public to take certain precautionary steps including boiling water for one minute before use by young children and immuno-compromised people. The water authority took urgent steps to remove the organisms from the water and tests over the last few days indicate that there has been a substantial improvement in the water leaving the works. Thames Water cannot yet be certain that there are none of these organisms left in the water and it is, therefore, maintaining the advice to boil water for the time being.

I understand that Thames Water also proposes to undertake an independently led review at learning lessons from the experience.

I am entirely satisfied that Thames Water has behaved in a very responsible manner throughout this incident and is taking all the necessary steps

Until 1985 there had been no confirmed connection anywhere in the world between cryptosporidiosis and water supplies. However, it is extremely difficult to detect the organism and complex new analytical techniques are only now being developed. Thames Water is in the forefront of these developments. For both these reasons, there is no routine sampling for this organism in water supplies.

Mr. Simon Coombs: To ask the Secretary of State for the Environment

(1)    if he will make a statement on the response of the Thames water authority to the possible threat to the public water supply in the Swindon area from the organism cryptosporidia;

(2)    what information he has on routine testing by water authorities for the organism cryptosporidia in the public water supply; and if he will make a statement;

(3)    what information he has on the incidence of the organism cryptosporidia, in the public water supply; and if he will make a statement.

Mr. Moynihan: I refer my hon. Friend to the answer given today by my hon. and learned Friend the Minister for Water and Planning to the hon. Member for Oxford East (Mr. Smith).

2 March 1989

CRYPTOSPORIDIA

Mr. Raffan: To ask the Secretary of State for the Environment whether the Government will be taking any further steps in respect of cryptosporidia in water supplies.

Mr. Howard: Thames Water has been dealing with a problem relating to cryptosporidia in water supplies in the Oxford and Swindon area. As a precaution, Thames Water extended special sampling to other parts of its area and by the end of last week a number of the organisms had been identified intermittently at some other water treatment works. However, no link has been established between currently reported cases of cryptosporidiosis and drinking water supplies outside the Oxford and Swindon areas and the Department of Health has advised that there is no need for consumers to take any special precautions. Thames Water is taking action aimed at removing the organisms from these additional supplies and will continue with intensive sampling. They also propose to undertake an independently led review aimed at learning lessons from the experience. This information was announced in a press release by Thames Water last Saturday.

In view of the absence of information on cryptosporidia in water supplies, my right hon. Friend the Secretary of State for the Environment, in consultation with my right hon. Friend the Secretary of State for Health, has decided to establish a group of experts under the chairmanship of Sir John Badenoch to advise on the subject. The group will consider the extent to which this organism may be present in water supplies, the monitoring methods necessary to detect it, the public health significance of its presence and whether any action is necessary.

EXPERT GROUP ON CRYPTOSPORIDIUM IN WATER SUPPLIES

TERMS OF REFERENCE

1.    To examine the occurrence and extent of Cryptosporidium in water supplies.

2.    To assess the significance for public health of Cryptosporidium in water supplies.

3.    To assess methods of monitoring for Cryptosporidium and to formulate advice to water undertakers upon monitoring strategy.

4.    To consider and formulate advice upon the protection of water supplies, treatment processes and the maintenance of distribution systems.

5.    To report jointly to the Secretary of State for the Environment and the Secretary of State for Health, and to produce an interim report by the end of June 1989.

## CRYPTOSPORIDIUM

*Cryptosporidium* species are minute parasites which can infect the gut of cattle, wild and domestic animals and man. Infection causes diarrhoea which occurs mainly in the very young, such as in calves and lambs. Most human cases are reported in children under 5 years old where it may be serious if not treated promptly. Normally in man, the disease is self-limiting and usually clears within 2 weeks but in AIDS patients and other immuno-compromised persons, it can be life-threatening.

The disease is spread by the oocysts of the parasite. These are minute, spherical bodies about 5 μm diameter, which are passed in the faeces and which survive for long periods in soil and water and are extremely resistant to most chemical disinfectants. Heat treatment, by boiling water or pasteurising foods, will kill the cysts. They are also killed by freezing of foods to below −20°C for 30 minutes. Normal chlorination of drinking water is ineffective. Indeed experiments conducted for WRc by the Scottish Parasite Reference Unit (SPRU) at Stobhill General Hospital, Glasgow on behalf of WRc have shown that treatment with 10,000–16,000 mg of free chlorine per litre is needed to destroy viability of the cysts. The cysts do not multiply in the environment.

*Cryptosporidium* species have been known for the past 80 years as parasites of cattle and of wild animals. They are able to infect a wide range of animal hosts including calves, lambs, piglets, poultry, rodent and domestic pets. The first human cases were reported in 1976. Since about 1982 the rate of detection of cryptosporidiosis in man has increased greatly, because of improved methods of detection and increased vigilance. These new methods are able to distinguish between these parasitic cysts and those which normally occur as harmless commensals in the human gut. Cryptosporidium is now recognised as a significant but nevertheless minor cause of human gastro-enteritis. It is thought that the main route of transmission in man is person-to-person, less commonly food or environmental contamination and that bovine strains are mainly involved.

The development in the last few years of precise serological methods for identifying the cysts and for determining infection is now indicating the extent of the disease and the distribution of the cysts in the environment, although there are still many gaps in knowledge. A high proportion of cattle have been shown to carry antibodies showing that at some period in their life they have been exposed to infection. Studies in the United States have shown that the cysts can be found in most waters and soils, although in small numbers.

The first outbreak of cryptosporidiosis to be associated with a water supply occurred in San Antonio, Texas in 1984.

The first outbreak in the UK confirmed to be associated with public water supply occurred in Ayrshire, in 1988 when the cause was identified as contamination of a break tank by land drainage off grassland, to which slurry had been applied. The exact cause of the present outbreak in the Swindon-Oxford area is undetermined, although cysts have been isolated from the filters at the waterworks.

Two further outbreaks associated with other types of water have been reported. One cluster of cases in North Wales was associated with a variety of environmental causes including recreational lakes subject to organic pollution. A further outbreak occurred at a public swimming pool in Yorkshire.

Water supply practices offer several barriers to the spread of this parasite. Treatment by storage in reservoirs after abstraction enables the cysts to be removed by sedimentation. A further safeguard occurs in the case of upland waters of high purity, where it is normal to exclude the public and farm animals from the margins of reservoirs. The processes of slow-sand filtration and of flocculation, coagulation and rapid sand filtration are effective in removing the cysts of parasitic protozoa, such as *Cryptosporidium, Giardia* and *Entamoeba histolytica*. It is to be expected, however, that cysts of *Cryptosporidium* and of other parasites will be found in the solids removed by filtration and adhering to the filtration medium, if they are present in the water being treated. From what has been said above it must be expected that small numbers of cryptosporidial cysts will be present in most natural waters, particularly after heavy rainfall and at times when certain livestock activities and slurry spreading are occurring.

WRc has sponsored further research at SPRL to examine further the effect of disinfectants upon the viability of the cysts of *Cryptosporidium* and to determine the effects of flocculation, coagulation and filtration and the ways in which these processes are operated upon their efficiency in removing the cysts. Although routine procedures are now available for filtering large volumes of water (in excess of 500 litres) and concentrating the cysts the final stages of isolation require specialist facilities (density-gradient centrifugation and fluorescence microscopy using monoclonal antibodies) which are only available at a few centres of expertise.

DOE Reference: WS/34/15/5
Welsh Office Reference: WEP/93/74/1                                    24 August 1989

To:     Chief Executives of Water Authorities and Secretaries of Water Companies in
        England and Wales


Dear Sir,

## CRYPTOSPORIDIUM IN WATER SUPPLIES

1.      Water Policy letter WP/6/1989 of 22 March 1989 provided water undertakers with
information and provisional advice on cryptosporidium in water supplies and referred to
the setting up of a Group of Experts under the Chairmanship of Sir John Badenoch to
advise on the subject. This letter provides further information and advice.

2.      On 25 July, Sir John wrote to the Secretaries of State for Environment and Health
to make an interim report on behalf of the Group of Experts. A copy of the letter is at
Annex A and the text of the Answer given by Michael Howard to a Parliamentary
Question from David Ashby MP announcing the interim report is at Annex B. You will
note from the Answer that the Secretaries of State have welcomed the report and have
undertaken to inform organisations which may have an interest in its findings.

3.      The main recommendations of the interim report which have a bearing on water
undertakers' operations are as follows:

(i)     Routine monitoring for cryptosporidium is not advocated but water undertakers
should initiate monitoring of water used in the treatment processes when a treatment
works is under strain or there has been significant change in operating procedures. Under
similar operating conditions the monitoring of water passing into supply should be
considered.

(ii)    If significant numbers of the organism are detected in such circumstances, treatment
works operations should be adjusted to prevent recycling of the organism.

(iii)   If the organism is found in treated water passing to supply, the operation of the
treatment works should be reviewed and the appropriate medical authorities informed.

(iv)    Undertakers should develop a capacity to monitor for the organism and should
ensure that they have access to a laboratory which has the necessary expertise for its
isolation and identification.

(v)     Standards of maintenance and repair of distribution systems, including service
reservoirs, should be of a high order. Steps should be taken to minimise surges in the flow
of water to treatment works and control measures, which are discussed in the Report,
should be adopted.

(vi)    There is no evidence to suggest that the use of either aluminium or iron compounds
in flocculation processes is superior in entrapping the oocysts of cryptosporidium.

(vii)   A co-ordinated programme of research is needed for gathering information about the occurrence of cryposporidium and the capacity of water treatment works to remove it or render it harmless.

(viii)   Close collaboration and arrangements for exchange of information should be developed between water undertakers, local authorities and health authorities to ensure that waterborne disease is kept under control.

4.   The Department and the Welsh Office endorse these recommendations but in so doing recognise that, until the Expert Group have completed their studies, there will be uncertainty over the action water undertakers might take in the different circumstances considered in the interim report. The Department and the Welsh Office will therefore arrange discussions with the Water Authorities Association and Water Companies' Association shortly with a view to clarifying the steps, if any, which water undertakers should take while the studies are still underway. Discussions have already been held with the Associations, the Water Research Centre and other Government Departments about the co-ordination of research and further discussions are planned.

5.   Any queries on this letter should be directed in England to Mr O D Hydes (Room A4.39, Telephone 01-276 8213), and in Wales to Mr J E Saunders, Water Division, Welsh Office, Cathays Park, Cardiff CF1 3NQ (Telephone (0222) 823178).

6.   Copies of this letter are being sent to the Secretaries of the Water Authorities Association and Water Companies' Association; the Chief Medical Officer, Department of Health; the Director of the Public Health Laboratory Service; the Chief Engineer, Civil Engineering and Water Services Directorate, Scottish Development Department; the Assistant Secretary, Water Services Division, Department of the Environment for Northern Ireland; the Heads of the Land Drainage, Fisheries and Food Safety Divisions of MAFF; and the Managing Director of the Water Research Centre. Copies of Sir John's letter will also go to the Local Authority Associations.

Yours faithfully



M G HEALEY                              A H H JONES
Drinking Water Division                 Water Divison
Department of the Environment           Welsh Office

Department of the Environment
Group of Experts on
Cryptosporidium in Water Supplies
A4.11 Romney House,
43 Marsham Street,
London SW1P 3PY

Telephone: 01-276 8282

The Rt Hon Christopher Patten MP                                    25 July 1989
Secretary of State for the Environment
2 Marsham Street
London SW1P 3EB

The Rt Hon Kenneth Clarke QC MP
The Secretary of State for Health
Richmond House
79 Whitehall
London SW1A 2NS

Dear Secretaries of State

PROGRESS REPORT ON THE WORK OF THE DoE GROUP OF EXPERTS ON
CRYPTOSPORIDIUM IN WATER SUPPLIES

On 2 March 1989 following an outbreak of cryptosporidiosis in that part of Oxfordshire
and Swindon supplied by water from the Farmoor Reservoir, Michael Howard, QC MP
Minister for Water and Planning, announced that an expert group had been set up, in
consultation with the Department of Health, to advise the Government on the significance
of cryptosporidium in water supplies. The names of the members of the group are
attached at Appendix A.

The group was given the following terms of reference:

(i)     To examine the occurrence and extent of cryptosporidium in water supplies;

(ii)    To assess the significance for public health of cryptosporidium in water supplies;

(iii)   To assess methods of monitoring for cryptosporidium and to formulate advice to
water undertakers upon monitoring strategies;

(iv)    To consider and formulate advice upon the protection of water supplies, treatment
processes and the maintenance of distribution systems;

(v)     To report jointly to the Secretary of State for the Environment and the Secretary of
State for Health and to produce an interim report by the end of July 1989.

From the outset it was clear that an assessment of the prevalence of cryptosporidium in
water systems throughout the country, and therefore its significance as a waterborne
pathogen for man, could not be made without further study. Further information was also
needed about the ways in which the organisms gain entry into the water supplies and on
the efficiency of water treatment processes in removing them. Some of the work is in hand
and other projects are being planned. We consider that the most useful way to acquire the
necessary information is through an adequately financed nationally co-ordinated
programme of research by water undertakers, the Public Health Laboratory Service, other
research organisations and Government departments.

This letter represents our interim report on measures that can be taken now to safeguard water supplies and discharges our remit to respond by the end of July. It also provides guidance on public health aspects of infection with cryptosporidium.

Later, we propose to report more extensively on the medical aspects of cryptosporidiosis and to formulate further interim guidance for water undertakers. This will be followed by a final report on the extent and significance of contamination of water supplies by cryptosporidium and on the methods which can be used for its control.

To date the group has held six meetings. It has taken oral evidence and studied a large number of scientific and technical papers.

I am greatly indebted to my colleagues for giving so much time and effort to the work of the group and to the Secretariat from the Department of Environment and the Department of Health for generous and effective support.

## CRYPTOSPORIDIUM IN WATER SUPPLIES

The organism cryptosporidium has a worldwide distribution. Although it has long been recognised as a parasite of animals, it was not until 1976 – a little over a decade ago – that it was shown to be capable of producing illness in man. Infected animals including man excrete the organism in their faeces in the form of minute oocysts which may cause infection if they are ingested.

Because of the organism's widespread distribution it must be assumed that from time to time oocysts will be present in all surface waters, including springs and shallow wells, and will be found intermittently in the effluent from sewage treatment works. Ground water from deep walls should theoretically be free from cryptosporidium but to confirm this further evidence is needed. Current methods of water treatment and disinfection properly carried out cannot eliminate entirely the risk of cryptosporidium passing into the water supply.

## ADVICE ON WATER TREATMENT

In the past, water undertakers had no reason to develop the capacity to test for cryptosporidium because it was not perceived as a public health risk. However, in the light of increasing knowledge of its role as a human pathogen they should now develop the capacity to monitor for it and ensure that they have access to a laboratory which has the necessary expertise for its isolation and identification.

The oocysts of cryptosporidia are difficult to kill. In particular they are unaffected by chlorine in the concentrations that can be used to treat drinking water. It is important that the use of ozone and other potentially effective disinfectants should be explored.

In water treatment, there is no evidence to suggest that the use of either aluminium or iron compounds in flocculation processes is superior in entrapping the oocysts of cryptosporidium.

Care should be taken in the operation of filter beds to avoid sudden surges of flow which may dislodge deposits including cryptosporidia. The use of turbidity meters, ideally on individual filter bed outlets, would provide a sensitive indication that such a surge has occurred and also indicate when a filter has been penetrated by particulate matter; their use is recommended.

In line with the advice given in the Department of the Environment's letter to water undertakers of 22 March 1989, we do not advocate routine monitoring for cryptosporidium in water supplies.

Cryptosporidium is most likely to be present in water sources in the spring and autumn. At these times of the year, when a treatment works is under strain, as in conditions of high throughput or when there has been a significant change in operating procedures, the water which has been used in the treatment process should be monitored. (This includes principally the water used for washing filters, and water associated with sludge from the flocculation process.) If oocysts of cryptosporidia are found in significant numbers, the disposal of this water whould be carefully controlled and it should not be returned to the waterworks inlets untreated. Under similar operating conditions monitoring of the final drinking water should also be considered. If oocysts are found, the operation of the works should be reviewed, and the appropriate medical authorities informed.

It is important that the water industry maintains high standards in the maintenance and repair of distribution systems including service reservoirs to reduce the risk of contamination by oocysts of cryptosporidium.

Even in the most carefully regulated and supervised systems, occasional emergencies may arise when temporarily the water supply is considered unfit for drinking. Non-domestic users of water, especially hospitals, and including industrial users and members of the retail trade for food and drink should consider how they would respond to the notice of an emergency being declared.

Water undertakers should develop a close collaboration with local authorities and health authorities. They should develop arrangements for the regular exchange of information so that they can respond to a possible incident of waterborne disease. The importance of close collaboration is reinforced by the fact that first indication of a possible waterborne outbreak of cryptosporidiosis is likely to be a report to the Medical Officer for Environmental Health (MOEH) that there has been a sudden increase in the number of cases.

PUBLIC HEALTH ASPECTS OF CRYPTOSPORIDIOSIS

Although giving advice on matters of public health is not strictly within our terms of reference we thought this should be included in our interim report.

In man cryptosporidiosis is usually characterised by a self-limiting illness with diarrhoea, abdominal cramps, vomiting and sometimes fever that resolves in one to three weeks. It can affect persons of any age but is most common in children between the ages of one and five years. In patients with AIDS and others whose resistance to infection is impaired, it is much more serious and may lead to severe and lasting disability.

It is not a common cause of diarrhoea. National reporting began in 1984: between 1984 and 1988 the annual number of recorded cases in England, Wales and Northern Ireland varied between 1,700 and 3,500 but this is almost certainly an underestimate of the actual number. A study by the Public Health Laboratory Service showed that only between 1% and 5% of all cases of diarrhoea which were confirmed by stool culture were due to cryptosporidium.

The disease is contracted by ingestion of the infective oocysts and develops after an incubation period of usually 3 to 11 days, but which can be as long as 25 days.

It is spread by direct or indirect contact with the faeces of an infected person or animal. It passes readily from person to person, in the family, play groups or nursery schools and other institutions.

Those in contact with farm animals such as farmers, visitors to farms, veterinarians and workers in abattoirs are also at risk and need to take appropriate precautions. Domestic pets can spread the infection but the risk from them appears to be less than that from farm animals.

84

Medical staff and others caring for patients with cryptosporidiosis should be aware of the risk of contacting the infection and that cryptosporidiosis is one of the recognised causes of travellers' diarrhoea.

Spread from person to person and from animals to man can be minimised by strict attention to personal hygiene with routine washing of hands especially before eating and after using the lavatory.

Cases of diarrhoea occurring in play groups or nurseries or in school children, particularly those who have recently visited farms or have been in contact with young farm animals, should be reported to the MOEH without delay.

There is a potential risk that raw milk could become contaminated by cryptosporidia and the public are advised not to drink milk unless it has been pasteurised.

It is probable that cryptosporidia are present in small numbers from time to time in all surface waters, including springs and streams. It is our advice that the public should not drink from these.

## CRYPTOSPORIDIOSIS AND DRINKING WATER SUPPLIES

Outbreaks of cryptosporidiosis due to contamination of drinking water supplies have been reported only rarely. To date there have only been six proven outbreaks: three in the United States of America and three in the United Kingdom.

An individual is much more likely to contract the infection if he comes into direct contact with the faeces of an infected person or animal. But the importance of contamination of the water suply is the potential that exists of giving rise to a very large number of cases. Where there has been an unusual incident involving gross contamination of the source of the water, existing water treatment procedures can not prevent cryptosporidia passing into the water supply.

When our studies are complete we will be reporting on measures designed to control the effects of such accidental contamination. In the interim surveillance should be continued by the water, local and health authorities, who will be responsible for advising the public should additional measures be required to safeguard drinking water.

We have received considerable help from the Scottish Home and Health Department and from other colleagues in Scotland. I am therefore copying this letter to the Secretary of State for Scotland.


Sir John Badenoch

DoE GROUP OF EXPERTS ON CRYPTOSPORIDIUM IN WATER SUPPLIES

**CHAIRMAN**
Sir John Badenoch MA DM FRCP FRCP
  (Ed)

**MEMBERS**

| | |
|---|---|
| Dr Chris Bartlett MSc MB FFCM | Public Health Laboratory Service |
| Dr Catherine Benton BSc PhD MIWEM CBiol | Strathclyde Regional Council |
| Dr Richard Cawthorne BVM & S Dip Biol PhD MRCVS | Ministry of Agriculture, Fisheries and Food |
| Mr Frank Earnshaw FICE MIMechE FIWEM | Severn Trent Water Authority |
| Professor Ken Ives DSc(Eng) FEng FICE | University College London |
| Mr Jack Jeffery MSc FIWEN FRIPHH | North Surrey Water Company |
| Dr Michael Vaile MB BS MRCGP FFCM | Director of Public Health Medicine, Maidstone Health Authority |
| Professor David Warrell MA DM FRCP | John Radcliffe Hospital |
| Dr A. E. Wright TD MD FRCPath DPH Dip Bact | Former Director, Public Health Laboratory, Newcastle upon Tyne |

**OBSERVERS**

| | |
|---|---|
| Mr Roy Cunningham | Department of Health |
| Dr Gerry Forbes FRACMA FACOM FREHIS MFCM LRCS & P DPH DIH DTM & H DMSA | Scottish Home and Health Department |
| Mr Michael Healey | Department of Environment |

**SECRETARIAT**

| | |
|---|---|
| Dr Ann Dawson BA MSc MRCP | Department of Health |
| Dr Derek Miller BSc PhD FIWEM MIChE | Water Research Centre |
| Mr Christopher Whaley | Department of Environment |

HOUSE OF COMMONS

Mr David Ashby (Con – North West Leicestershire);

551. To ask the Secretary of State for the Environment whether he has received the report of the Group of Experts on Cryptosporidium in Water Supplies and will he make a statement.


MR MICHAEL HOWARD

Sir John Badenoch, Chairman of the Group of Experts, wrote to my rt hon and learned Friend the Secretary of State for Health and my rt hon Friend the Secretary of State for the Environment on 25 July 1989 to present the Group's interim report. Copies of the letter have been placed in the Library. The establishment of the Group was announced on 2 March 1989 (Official Report 148, Col 286) and an interim report was requested by the end of July.

The interim report says that the organism cryptosporidium has a world-wide distribution. Although it has long been recognised as a parasite of animals, it was not until 1976 – a little over a decade ago – that it was shown to be capable of producing illness in man. Infected animals including man excrete the organism in their faeces in the form of minute oocysts which may cause infection if they are ingested.

In man cryptosporidiosis is usually characterised by a self-limiting illness with diarrhoea, abdominal cramps, vomiting and sometimes fever that resolves in one to three weeks. It can affect persons of any age but is most common in children between the ages of one and five years. In patients with AIDS and others whose resistance to infection is impaired, it is much more serious and may lead to severe and lasting disability.

Because of the organism's widespread distribution, the Group indicate that it must be assumed that, from time to time, oocysts will be present in all surface waters including springs and shallow wells. Current methods of water treatment and disinfection properly carried out cannot eliminate entirely the risk of cryptosporidium passing into the water supply.

However, though the Group recognise the potential that exists for giving rise to a very large number of cases through public water supplies they point out that an individual is much more likely to contract the infection if he comes into direct contact with the faeces of an infected person or animal.

The letter points to the need for high standards of maintenance and repair of water distribution systems, for extra monitoring at water treatment works in certain circumstances and for some modification of operating procedures should the organism be detected in significant numbers. Close collaboration between water undertakers, local authorities and health authorities is advocated. A co-ordinated programme of research is proposed for gathering information upon the occurrence of cryptosporidium and the capacity of water treatment works to remove it.

I am advised that the Expert Group have spent considerable time examining the more general public health aspects of cryptosporidiosis and will make a fuller report in due course. In their interim report they identify those most at risk from contracting the disease and they put forward simple precautions for prevention.

My rt hon Friends welcome the interim report and are grateful to Sir John and his colleagues for the considerable effort they have made so far in undertaking this study. The Departments will draw the attention of water undertakers, local authorities, health authorities and other organisations to the interim conclusions and recommendations. Ways of undertaking the proposed research are already under consideration.

Friday 28 July 1989                                                                5207/88/89
Department of the Environment

DOE/Welsh Office
WP/17/1989                                                     29 September 1989

DOE Reference: WS/35/1/1
Welsh Office Reference: WEP/32/12/9

To: Chief Executives of Water Services Companies and Secretaries of Water Companies in England and Wales

Dear Sir,

LEAD IN DRINKING WATER

1.    The purpose of this letter is to inform you of recent medical advice on the health risks from lead in drinking water.

2.    The significance of exposure to lead from all sources was reassessed in the report of the Medical Research Council's (MRC) Advisory Group on Lead and Neuropsychological Effects in Children[1] of June 1988. The Group concluded that it would be prudent to continue to reduce the environmental lead to which children are exposed.

3.    The implications of the MRC report for lead in drinking water were subsequently considered by the Department of Health's independent expert advisory Committee on the Medical Aspects of the Contamination of Air, Soil and Water (CASW). As a result of that consideration the Committee:

(i)    expressed concern that some people may be exposed to concentrations of 100μg lead/l in drinking water, or higher concentrations;

(ii)    recommended that a limit of 50μg lead/l should be introduced as a practical measure to identify areas where further action to reduce lead concentrations is a priority;

(iii)    advised that the aim in the long term should be to achieve compatibility both with the criterion that in not more than 2% of the population of interest should the blood lead concentration exceed 25μg/dl, and with a weekly intake of not more than 25μg lead per kg body weight in infants and children.

---

[1]    The Neuropsychological Effects of Lead in Children: A Review of the Research 1984–1988 available from the Publications Section, Medical Research Council, 20 Park Crescent, London W1N 4AC

The bases for the figures in (iii) are the Department of Health's longstanding recommendation that action should be taken to reduce exposure to lead where a person, particularly a child has a blood lead level of over 25 $\mu$g/dl, and the recommendation of the FAO/WHO Joint Expert Committee on Food Additives (JECFA) of a provisional tolerable weekly lead intake (PTWI) of not more than 25 $\mu$g per body weight in infants and children.

4.     The advice of the MRC Advisory Group and CASW and JECFA's PTWI have all been accepted and endorsed by the Chief Medical Officer. As a consequence the Water Supply (Water Quality) Regulations 1989 set more stringent requirements than does the EC Drinking Water Directive. The lead standard in the Regulations is 50 $\mu$g/l in any sample and the ambiguous comments in the Directive relating to flushed samples and 100 $\mu$g lead/l have not been included in the Regulations. The Regulations place new responsibilities on water undertakers. Whenever there is a risk that the standard may be exceeded in a water supply zone they are required to treat the water except where;

a)     the treatment is unlikely to achieve a significant reduction in the concentration of lead;

or   b)     the prescribed risk relates only to water supplied in an insignificant part of the zone;

or   c)     treatment is not reasonably practical.

The undertaker has duty to remove its part of a lead pipe where the remainder of that lead pipe connecting to a drinking water tap under mains pressure has been removed and the owner of the premises has requested the undertaker in writing to remove its lead pipe.

5.     Guidance on the implementation of these responsibilities is set out in the document 'Guidance on Safeguarding the Quality of Public Water Supplies' now being published. This states that a risk should be presumed in all water supply zones unless there is clear evidence to the contrary.

6.     In the light of the new medical advice referred to in this letter the Government is considering whether further action is needed in a wider context.

7.     Any queries on this letter should be directed in England to Owen Hydes, Department of the Environment, Room A4.39, Romney House, 43 Marsham Street, London SW1P 3PY (telephone 01-276 8213) and in Wales to John Saunders, Water Division, Welsh Office, Room 2117, Cathays Park, Cardiff, CF1 3NQ, (telephone 0222 823 178).

8.     Copies of this letter are being sent to the Secretaries of the Water Services Association and the Water Companies' Association; the Chief Engineer, Civil Engineering and Water Services Directorate, Scottish Development Department; the Assistant Secretary, Water Service Division, Department of the Environment for Northern Ireland; the Heads of the Land Drainage and Fisheries Divisions of MAFF; the Government's Chief Medical Officer and the Managing Director of the Water Research Centre.

Yours faithfully


M. G. HEALEY                          A. H. H. JONES
Drinking Water Division               Water Division
Department of the Environment         Welsh Office

DOE/WELSH OFFICE                                        29 September 1989

WP 18/1989

DOE Reference: WS/45/1/1
Welsh Office Reference: WEP 8/55/1

To: Chief Executives of Water Service Companies and Secretaries of Water Companies in England and Wales

Dear Sir,

PESTICIDES IN WATER SUPPLIES

1.     This letter provides guidance and information about those pesticides which are widely used and have been or are likely to be detected in water supplies. It supplements the advice given in 'Guidance on Safeguarding the Quality of Water Supplies' (the Guidance Document) now being published by the Departments. It supersedes the advice given in Water Policy letter WP10/1986.

2.     The Guidance Document advises each water undertaker to develop a monitoring strategy for pesticides based on the likely risk of particular pesticides being present in a water source serving a water supply zone by:

(a)     assessing which pesticides are used in significant amounts within the catchment area; and

(b)     assessing on the basis of the properties and use of these pesticides whether any is likely to reach a water source in the catchment.

3.     The appendix to this letter gives information on those pesticides which are most widely used in agriculture and horticulture and in non-agricultural situations and have been or are likely to be detected in water supplies. It includes information on usage, solubility and persistence in soil and water and on methods of analysis. This information should assist water undertakers with the development of their monitoring strategy.

4.     The Guidance Document also advises water undertakers on the action to be taken when a pesticide concentration in the water leaving a treatment works or in distribution:

(a)     exceeds the standard of 0.1 $\mu$g/l prescribed in the Water Supply (Water Quality) Regulations 1989; and

(b)     exceeds the standard but also approaches or exceeds the advisory value for that pesticide.

A table of advisory values is given in the Guidance Document.

5.    The appendix to this letter explains the derivation of the advisory values and their interpretation. They will be reviewed as new data become available. It should be noted that the values err very considerably on the side of safety and that they are provided as signals for water undertakers to take the action advised in the Guidance Document. However, the advisory values are not to be interpreted as maximum acceptable concentrations. Where an advisory value is exceeded the Department or Welsh Office should also be consulted on the action to be taken.

6.    Any queries on this letter should be directed in England to Owen Hydes, Department of the Environment, Room A4.39, Romney House, 43 Marsham Street, London SW1P 3PY (telephone 01-276 8213) and in Wales to John Saunders, Water Division, Welsh Office, Room 2117, Cathays Park, Cardiff, CF1 3NQ, (telephone 0222 823 178).

7.    Copies of this letter are being sent to the Secretaries of the Water Services Association and the Water Companies' Association; the Chief Engineer, Civil Engineering and Water Services Directorate, Scottish Development Department; the Assistant Secretary, Water Service Division, Department of the Environment for Northern Ireland; the Heads of the Land Drainage, Fisheries and Pesticide Safety Divisions of MAFF; the Government's Chief Medical Officer; the Chief Executive of the National Rivers Authority and the Managing Director of the Water Research Centre.


Yours faithfully


M.G. HEALEY                          A H H JONES
Drinking Water Division              Water Division
Department of the Environment        Welsh Office

# APPENDIX

This appendix provides information on those pesticides which:

(a)  are most widely used in agriculture and horticulture and in non-agricultural situations;

(b)  have been detected in water sources and supplies; and

(c)  could be detected in some water sources and supplies because of their characteristics.

## A  *Pesticide Usage*

A.1 The attached table gives the estimated annual usage in tonnes of individual pesticides used in agriculture and horticulture. It has been compiled from MAFF Survey Report 41, Review of Usage of Pesticides in Agriculture and Horticulture in England and Wales 1980–83. Some formulations contain more than one active ingredient: to calculate the total amount of individual pesticide used it has been assumed that mixtures contain equal amounts of active ingredients.

A.2 When the 1980–83 data are compared with 1975–79 data it can be seen that there have been some very significant changes in the use of some individual pesticides. There are likely to have been further significant changes in pesticide usage since 1980–83. This shows the importance of water undertakers' establishing periodically which pesticides are used in their catchments through liaison with the Agricultural Development Advisory Service.

A.3 No recent collated information is available on the non-agricultural uses of pesticides. The Department of the Environment has, therefore, commissioned a survey, which is currently being undertaken. One of the main non-agricultural uses is that of herbicides by local authorities, public utilities and nationalised and commercial industries. The principal pesticides used are **sodium chlorate, atrazine** and **simazine,** each at a rate of several hundred tonnes of active ingredient per annum in England and Wales.

## B  *Solubility of Pesticides*

B.1 The table gives the solubility in mg/l of individual pesticides obtained from the literature. The solubility of most of the pesticides listed exceeds 0.1 μg/l and, in some cases, the advisory value also. Apart from **sulphur** and **tar oil,** which are considered unlikely to reach water supplies, the pesticides which are quoted as insoluble or practically insoluble are included in the table because they have salts which are soluble (**ioxynil, bromoxynil** and **2,4-D)** or are believed to have sufficient solubility to give concentrations greater than 0.1 μg/l.

B.2 More important factors than solubility in determining whether a pesticide is likely to reach a water source are its persistence in soil and water and whether it is transferred from the soil to water. These factors are considered in Section C.


## C  Persistence and Degradability of Pesticides in Soil and Water

C.1 Information on the persistence and degradability of pesticides in soil and water has been provided by MAFF from literature surveys. Most of this information relates to pesticides in soils and generally more information is available for the more recently developed pesticides. Provision of information on persistence in soil and water and transfer from soil to water is now required under the Control of Pesticides Regulations (COPR) 1986, before approval for the sale of pesticides will be given.

C.2 The information is available in a non-standard form which makes comparisons between pesticides difficult. Persistence and degradability depend on many factors, for example: formulation and method of application; type of soil (sandy, peaty, clay); and conditions such as temperature and pH value. For these reasons the table gives a description of the persistence of the pesticide rather than absolute data. The terms used are defined as follows–

| | |
|---|---|
| readily degraded | – most disappears within days |
| degraded | – most disappears within weeks |
| fairly persistent | – most remains for months |
| persistent | – most remains for over a year |
| no inf | – no information (sometimes an estimate based on chemical structure is given) |

These terms may be qualified where appropriate.


## D  Advisory Values

D.1 The advisory values in the table have been derived in several ways. For three pesticides (the herbicides – **atrazine, MCPA** and **simazine**) the World Health Organisation (WHO) has published 'guideline values' for drinking water (1). The calculations for each of these three started from the 'no-effect level' (NEL), which is the largest daily dose of the herbicide (in mg/kg body weight) which has been shown to produce no observed adverse effect in all mammalian species tested in long-term feeding studies. The NEL was divided by a 'safety factor' which was intended to allow for uncertainties in the basic data and the extrapolation from data on animals to man, and to incorporate a safety margin against the possibility of effects on specially vulnerable groups, such as babies, within the general population. For these three herbicides the 'safety factor' was 1000. The resulting figure is the 'acceptable daily intake' (ADI). The ADI was scaled up for a 70 kg person to give an intake in mg/day. 10% of this intake was allocated to drinking water, and it was assumed that 2 litres of drinking water would be consumed daily. The WHO document notes that the 10% allocation of dietary intake to drinking water is higher than that for substances included in the 1984 'Guidelines for Drinking Water Quality' (2) because residues of herbicides reviewed are unlikely to be present to any significant extent in food at the time of consumption. The resulting values have been rounded down to one significant figure to give the advisory values in the table.

D2. For several other pesticides, ADIs have been proposed at the joint meetings of the Food and Agriculture Organisation (FAO) Panel of Experts on Pesticides Residues in Food and the Environment and the WHO Expert Group on Food Residues (3).

D2.1 The advisory values for the herbicides, **2,4-D, glyphosate** and **paraquat** have been derived from these ADIs by the steps set out in the last four sentences of paragraph D1 above.

D2.2 The advisory values for those pesticides which are not herbicides, **aldrin/dieldrin, carbendazim, carbophenothion, chlordane, chlormequat, DDT, dimethoate, gamma-HCH, heptachlor/heptachlor epoxide, malathion, mancozeb, maneb, methoxychlor** and **triadimefon** have been derived from proposed ADIs (see paragraph D2) by the steps set out in the last four sentences of paragraph D1 above except that 1% of the intake in mg/day was allocated to drinking water. This reflects the basis of the calculations adopted for pesticides by WHO in their 1984 Guidelines (2).

D3. Where an ADI has not been proposed by WHO/FAO, NELs have been taken from the summary data published in the Agrochemicals Handbook (4) for the herbicides, **bromoxynil, carbetamide, chloridazon, clopyralid, dicamba, dichlorprop, difenzoquat, EPTC, ioxynil, isoproturon, linuron** and **metamitron** and in the Pesticide Manual (5) for the herbicides, **chlorotoluron, mecoprop, prometryn, propazine** and **triallate**. Where the data were reported only as mg/kg diet, they were converted to mg/kg body-weight for humans by dividing by 20 (for data from feeding studies in rats) or 40 (studies in dogs). Where more than one NEL was indicated for a pesticide, the lowest NEL was chosen. ADIs were then calculated using a safety factor of 1000, and subsequent steps were as set out in the last four sentences of paragraph D1 above.

D4. The advisory value for **MCPB** is identical to that for **MCPA,** which is structurally similar, and to which **MCPB** is converted in plants.

D5. The advisory value for **hexachlorobenzene** (HCB) is 0.2 $\mu$g/l. This is higher than the guideline value suggested by WHO. The 1984 (WHO) Guidelines (2) state that

'Two studies in mice and hamsters indicate that **HCB** is a carcinogen. Application of the linear multistage model for an additional cancer risk of 1 per 100,000 population per lifetime of exposure gives a recommended guideline value of 0.01 $\mu$g/l.'

The WHO guideline value, however, was also derived from water quality criteria for rivers, and included an allowance for exposure by eating fish. The higher advisory of 0.2$\mu$g/l value results from removal of this inappropriate allowance.

D6. Advisory values have not been derived for **metham sodium, methyl bromide, propyzamide, sodium chlorate** or **trichloroacetic acid** (TCA) because no appropriate data are available in the references given at the end of this section.

D7. The derivation of the advisory values is intended to provide a wide margin of safety. The presence in drinking water of a pesticide at a concentration at or lower than the advisory value should not represent a hazard to health, nor is it true that a concentration exceeding the advisory value necessarily renders the drinking water unsafe.

D8. The toxicological data on pesticides are subject to review. In particular, WHO has instituted a revision of its 1984 Guidelines for Drinking Water Quality (2) including an expanded list of pesticides. The advisory values will be revised as necessary in the light of any important relevant new information. Also the Government is pressing the European Commission for a review of the pesticide parameter in the EC Drinking Water Directive.

*References*

(1) World Health Organisation.
Drinking Water Quality – Guidelines for Selected Herbicides. (WHO Environmental Health Series 27). Copenhagen: WHO, 1987.

(2) World Health Organisation.
Guidelines for Drinking Water Quality. Vol 1 Recommendations.
Geneva, World Health Organisation, 1984.

(3) Food and Agriculture Organisation/World Health Organisation.
Reports of the Joint Meetings of the FAO Panel of Experts on Pesticide Residues in Food
and the Environment and the WHO Expert Group on Pesticide Residues 1962–1988.
Published as: WHO Technical Report Series, WHO/Food/Add, WHO Pesticide Series &
FAO Plant Production and Protection Papers.

(4) Royal Society of Chemistry.
Agrochemicals Handbook 2nd Edition.
Nottingham: Royal Society of Chemistry Information Services 1987 (updated to June
1989).

(5) Worthing C R (ed).
Pesticide Manual: a World Compendium 8th Edition.
Croydon, British Crop Protection Council, 1987.


E   *Analytical Methods*

The Standing Committee of Analysts (SCA) of the Department is responsible for
organising the development of analytical methods and for publishing the agreed methods.
The following list indicates the current position.

| Number | Method | ISBN number or status |
|---|---|---|
| 1. | Organochlorine insecticides and PCBs in water 1978 | 0 11 751373 3 |
| 2. | The determination of organochlorine insecticides and PCBs in sewage, sludges, muds and fish 1978, in water (an addition (1984)). | 0 11 751777 1 |
| 3. | Chlorobenzenes in water, organochlorine insecticides and PCBs in turbid waters, halogenated solvents and related compounds in sewage sludge and waters 1985. | 0 11 751913 8 |
| 4. | Organophosphorus pesticides in river and drinking water 1980 (tentative method). | 0 11 75660 0 |
| 5. | Organophosphorus pesticides in sewage sludge, in river and drinking water 1985. | 0 11 751912 X |
| 6. | Chlorophenoxyacidic herbicides, trichlorobenzoic acid, chlorophenols, triazines, and glyphosate in waters 1985. | 0 11 751886 7 |
| 7. | The determination of carbamates, thiocarbamates, related substances and ureas in water 1987. | 0 11 752151 5 |
| 8. | Determination of diquat and paraquat in river and drinking water, spectrophotometric methods (Tentative) 1987. | 0 11 752076 5 |
| 9. | Bromoxynil, ioxynil clopyralid and pentachlorophenol and esters in waters. | in draft |
| 10. | The determination of hydrocarbon oils in waters by solvent extraction, I R and gravimetry 1983. | 0 11 751728 3 |
| 11. | Determination of very low concentrations of hydrocarbons and halogenated hydrocarbons in water 1984. | 0 11 752004 7 |
| 12. | Sulphate in waters, effluents and solids 1979, second edition 1988. | 0 11 751492 6 / 0 11 752240 6 |

96

| Number | Method | ISBN number or status |
|--------|--------|-----------------------|
| 13. | The determination of anoins and cations, transition metals, and other complex ions and organic acids and bases by chromatography. | in draft |
| 14. | Benomyl, carbendazim, dinocap and dinoseb in waters | in draft |
| 15. | Chlormequat in water. | in draft |
| 16. | Chlortoluron, Isoproturon, linuron and diuron in water | in draft |
| 17. | Difenzoquat in water | in draft |
| 18. | Metamitron in water | in draft |
| 19. | Methane and other hydrocarbon gases in water 1988. | 0 11 752128 0 |
| 20. | Analysis of volatile trace organic substances in water by purge and trap techniques | in draft |
| 21. | Triadimefon, chlorthalonil and propyzamide in water | in draft |
| 22. | Dalapon and trichloroacetic acid in water | in draft |
| 23. | Analysis of hydrocarbons in water – A review, and an UV fluorescent spectrometric method 1988. | 0 11 752170 1 |
| 24. | Aldicarb, aminotriazole and chloridazon in water | in draft |

The following references may also be useful in the analysis of certain pesticides and the development of analytical methods.

| | |
|---|---|
| General booklet – high performance liquid chromatography, ion chromatography, thin layer and column chromatrography of water samples 1983 (detailed methods for specific substances will be developed as soon as possible). | 0 11 751726 7 |
| Pyrethrins and permethrin in potable waters by EC-GC 1981. | 0 11 751628 7 |
| Determination of synthetic pyrethroids in water effluents sewages, sludges, trade effluents, muds, fish and invertebrates. | in draft |
| The sampling of oils, fats, waxes and tars in aqueous and solid systems 1983. | 0 11 751956 1 |
| The determination of microgram and sub-microgram amounts of individual phenols in river and potable waters 1988. | 0 11 752099 3 |
| The tentative identification of volatilizable organic compounds by linear programmed gas chromatographic retention indices, with notes on other methods for identifying organic substances 1988. | 0 11 752222 8 |

The table quotes the reference number for the analytical method or methods appropriate for the particular pesticide. Further information on those methods still being developed and tested may be obtained from Mr L R Pittwell, Secretary of SCA, Department of the Environment, Room A438, Romney House, 43 Marsham Street, London SW1P 3PY; telephone 01 276-8298.

| PESTICIDE | MAIN TYPE/USE | USAGE (tonnes/a active ingredient) | SOLUBILITY IN WATER (mg/l) | (°C) | PERSISTENCE SOIL | WATER | COMMENTS | ADVISORY VALUE (µg/l) | ANALYTICAL METHOD SCA REF |
|---|---|---|---|---|---|---|---|---|---|
| Aldrin/ Dieldrin | Insecticide | No approval under COPR | 0.027 0.186 | 27 20 | Persistent | Persistent | Unlikely to reach water | 0.03 | (1,2,3) |
| Atrazine* | Herbicide - non agricultural | Several hundred | 33 | 20 | Fairly persistent Some leaching into water. | Fairly persistent | Likely to reach water - has been detected on many occasions. | 2 | (6) |
| Bromoxynil (mainly in mixtures) | Herbicide - cereals | 523 | 130 Octanoate salt (insol.) Sodium salt 42 x 10³ | 35 25 | Degraded Should not leach into water | No inf Probably persistent | Unlikely to reach water but needs to be checked. | 10 | (9) |
| Carbendazim | Fungicide - cereals | 489 | 29 | 20 | Persistent No inf on leaching | No inf Probably persistent | Likely to reach water | 3 | (14) |
| Carbeta- mide* | Selective herbicide | 72 | 3500 | 20 | Fairly persistent | Some degradation | Likely to reach water | 500 | (7) |
| Carbopheno- thion | Seed treatment cereals veterinary use | Very small | 0.34 | 20 | Fairly persistent No inf on leaching | No inf Probably persistent | May reach water | 0.1 | (4,5) |
| Chlordane (total isomers) | Insecticide | Very limited use | 0.1 | 25 | Persistent | Persistent | Unlikely to reach water | 0.1 | (1,2,3) |

* detected in water supplies at a concentration above 0.1 ug/l on at least one occasion during 1988

| PESTICIDE | MAIN TYPE/USE | USAGE (tonnes/a active ingredient) | SOLUBILITY IN WATER (mg/l) | (°C) | PERSISTENCE SOIL | PERSISTENCE WATER | COMMENTS | ADVISORY VALUE (µg/l) | ANALYTICAL METHOD SCA REF |
|---|---|---|---|---|---|---|---|---|---|
| Chloridazon | Herbicide - other arable | 247 | 400 | 20 | Degraded (4-amino-6-chloropyridazone metabolite) No inf on leaching | No inf Probably persistent | May reach water | 50 | (14,24) |
| Chlormequat | Growth regulator - cereals | 1053 | 1000 x 10³ | 25 | Degraded little leaching to lower soil layers | No inf Probably fairly persistent | Unlikely to reach water | 10 | (13,15) |
| Chlortoluron* | Herbicide - cereals | 1884 | 70 | 25 | Degraded (Substituted aniline metabolite) No inf on leaching | No inf Probably persistent | Likely to reach water - has been detected on some occasions. | 80 | (7, 16) |
| Clopyralid* | Herbicide | 228 | 9000 | 20 | Degraded No inf on leaching | Probably persistent | Likely to reach water | 100 | (9) |
| 2,4-D * | Herbicide | 81 | 620 | 25 | Degraded leaches into water | Some degradation | Likely to reach water | 1000 | (6) |
| DDT (total isomers) | Herbicide | no approval under COPR | practically insoluble | | Persistent | Persistent | Unlikely to reach water | 7 | (1,2,3) |
| Dicamba* | Herbicide - cereals | 202 | 6500 Sodium salt 360 x 10³ | 25 25 | Fairly persistent Leaches into water | No inf Probably persistent | Likely to reach water | 4 | (6) |
| Dichlorprop* | Herbicide - cereals | 332 | 350 Sodium salt 600 x 10³ | 20 20 | Degraded to dichlorophenol No inf on leaching | No inf Probably persistent | Likely to reach water | 40 | (6) |

* detected in water supplies at a concentration above 0.1 ug/l on at least one occasion during 1988

99

| PESTICIDE | MAIN TYPE/USE | USAGE (tonnes/a) (active ingredient) | SOLUBILITY IN WATER (mg/l) (°C) | PERSISTENCE | | | ADVISORY VALUE (ug/l) | ANALYTICAL METHOD SCA REF |
|---|---|---|---|---|---|---|---|---|
| | | | | SOIL | WATER | COMMENTS | | |
| Difenzoquat | Herbicide - cereals | 215 | Sodium salt $765 \times 10^3$  25 | Fairly persistent No inf on leaching | No inf Probably persistent | May reach water | 80 | (17) |
| Dimethoate* | Insecticide - cereals | 35 | Slightly soluble | Readily degraded Leaches rapidly from wet soil | Fairly persistent | Likely to reach water | 3 | (4, 5) |
| EPTC* | Pre-emergence herbicide | 28 | 375  24 | Fairly persistent No inf on leaching | Persistent | Likely to reach water | 50 | (7) |
| gamma HCH | Insecticide | Some use | 7  5 | Fairly persistent | Fairly persistent | May reach water | 3 | (1,2,3) |
| Glyphosate+ | Herbicide - cereals | 809 | Very soluble | Degraded Does not leach from soil | Degraded by microbial action | Unlikely to reach water | 1000 | (6) |
| Heptachlor/ Heptachlor epoxide | Insecticide | No approval under COPR | 0.056  25 | Persistent | Persistent | Unlikely to reach water | 0.1 | (1,2,3) |
| Hexachloro benzene | | No approval under COPR | Practically insoluble | Persistent | Persistent | Unlikely to reach water | 0.2 | (1,2,3) |
| Ioxynil (mainly in mixtures) | Herbicide - cereals | 634 | 50  25 Octanoate salt (insol.) Sodium salt $140 \times 10^3$ | Readily degraded No inf on leaching | No inf Probably persistent | May reach water | 10 | (9) |

* detected in water supplies at a concentration above 0.1 ug/l on at least one occasion during 1988

+ cleared for use in and near water courses.

| PESTICIDE | MAIN TYPE/USE | USAGE (tonnes/a) (active ingredient) | SOLUBILITY IN WATER (mg/l) | (°C) | PERSISTENCE SOIL | PERSISTENCE WATER | PERSISTENCE COMMENTS | ADVISORY VALUE (µg/l) | ANALYTICAL METHOD SCA REF |
|---|---|---|---|---|---|---|---|---|---|
| Isoproturon* | Herbicide - cereals | 1474 | 55 | 22 | Degraded No inf on leaching | No inf Probably persistent | Likely to reach water - has been detected on some occasions | 4 | (7, 16) |
| Linuron (mainly in mixtures)* | Herbicide - cereals | 393 | 75 | 25 | Fairly persistent microbial degradation. No inf on leaching. | No inf Probably fairly persistent | Likely to reach water | 10 | (7, 16) |
| Malathion* | Insecticide | 4 | 145 | 20 | Degraded No inf on leaching | Fairly persistent | Likely to reach water | 7 | (4,5) |
| Mancozeb (Maneb plus zinc oxide) | Fungicide - other arable | 263 | Practically insoluble | | Degraded to ethylene thiuram disulphide (ETD) and ethylene thiourea (ETU) No inf on leaching | No inf May degrade to ETD and ETU | Unlikely to reach water Degradation products might | 10 | (7) |
| Maneb (see Mancozeb) | Fungicide - cereals | 436 | Practically insoluble | | Degraded to ETD and ETU No inf on leaching | Probably degraded to ETD, ETM and ETU | Unlikely to reach water Degradation products might | 10 | (7) |
| MCPA* | Herbicide - cereals | 981 | 825 | 25 | Fairly persistent Degrades to 2-methyl-4-chloro phenol some leaching into water | No inf Probably persistent | Likely to reach water - has been detected on some occasions | 0.5 | (6) |

* detected in water supplies at a concentration above 0.1 ug/l on at least one occasion during 1988

| PESTICIDE | MAIN TYPE/USE | USAGE (tonnes/a) (active ingredient) | SOLUBILITY IN WATER (mg/l) | (°C) | PERSISTENCE | | | ADVISORY VALUE (µg/l) | ANALYTICAL METHOD SCA REF |
|---|---|---|---|---|---|---|---|---|---|
| | | | | | SOIL | WATER | COMMENTS | | |
| Oil | Herbicide – other arable | 396 | Practically insoluble | | No inf Probably degraded slowly. Probably not leached | No inf Probably persistent | Unlikely to reach water | 10 parameter A18 in Regulations | (10,11, 23) |
| Paraquat | Herbicide – cereals | 286 | Very soluble | | Strongly adsorbed and deactivated. Does not leach | Adsorbs onto solids | Unlikely to reach water | 10 | (8) |
| Prometryne* | Herbicide | 5 | 48 | 20 | Degraded No inf on leaching | Persistent | Likely to reach water | 10 | (6) |
| Propazine* | Herbicide | no approved uses | 9 | 20 | Fairly persistent | Fairly persistent | May reach water | 20 | (6) |
| Propyzamide* | Herbicide | 74 | 15 | 25 | Degraded little leaching | No inf | Likely to reach water | | |
| Simazine* | Herbicide – non agricultural | Several hundred | 5 | 20 | Fairly persistent little leaching | Fairly persistent | Likely to reach water – has been detected on many occasions | 10 | (6) |
| Sodium chlorate | Herbicide – non agricultural | Several hundred | 790 x10$^3$ | 0 | Fairly persistent No inf on leaching | No inf Probably persistent | May reach water | | (13) |
| Sulphur | Fungicide – other arable | 637 | Practically insoluble | | No inf Probably persistent unlikely to leach | No inf Probably persistent | Unlikely to reach water | Not necessary | |

* detected in water supplies at a concentration above 0.1ug/l on at least one occasion during 1988 (detection of propazine not confirmed).

+ since sodium chlorate is present in sodium hypochlorite which may be used as a disinfectant and may be formed in water as a reaction product from the use of chlorine dioxide in water treatment, confirmation that any significant concentrations found are due to the use of the pesticide is necessary by examination of the untreated water source.

| PESTICIDE | MAIN TYPE/USE | USAGE (tonnes/a) (active ingredient) | SOLUBILITY IN WATER (mg/l) | (°C) | PERSISTENCE SOIL | WATER | COMMENTS | ADVISORY VALUE (µg/l) | ANALYTICAL METHOD SCA REF |
|---|---|---|---|---|---|---|---|---|---|
| MCPB* | Herbicide - cereals | 76 | 44 | 25 | Fairly persistent Degrades like MCPA to 2-methyl - 4-chloro phenol | No inf | Likely to reach water | 0.5 | (6) |
| Mecoprop* | Herbicide - cereals | 3407 | 620 | 25 | Degraded No inf on leaching | No inf Probably persistent | Likely to reach water - has been detected on some occasions | 10 | (6) |
| Metamitron | Herbicide - other arable | 532 | 1800 | 20 | Degraded by deamination. Very little leaching from soil | No inf Probably persistent | Unlikely to reach water | 40 | (18) |
| Metham-sodium | Soil sterilant - other arable | 1230 | $722 \times 10^3$ | 20 | Readily degraded to methylisothio-cyanate (MITC) No inf on leaching | No inf Probably hydrolysed to MITC which is insoluble | Unlikely to reach water | | (7) |
| Methoxy-chlor | Insecticide | No approval under COPR | 0.1 | 25 | Persistent | Persistent | Unlikely to reach water | 30 | (1,2,3) |
| Methyl-bromide | Soil sterilant - protected crops | 393 | 13500 | 25 | Not persistent as it volatilises Degraded, bromide persists in soil | No inf Probably not persistent | Unlikely to reach water Bromide may be leached | | (19,20) |

* detected in water supplies at a concentration on at least one occasion during 1988

103

| PESTICIDE | MAIN TYPE/USE | USAGE (tonnes/a) (active ingredient) | SOLUBILITY IN WATER (mg/l) (°C) | PERSISTENCE | | COMMENTS | ADVISORY VALUE (ug/l) | ANALYTICAL METHOD SCA REF |
|---|---|---|---|---|---|---|---|---|
| | | | | SOIL | WATER | | | |
| Sulphuric acid | Herbicide - other arable | 6989 | Very soluble | Persistent Likely to leach | Persistent | Likely to reach water but no problem with EC Directive | Sulphate 250 mg/l Parameter A7 in Regulations | (12,13) |
| TCA+ (trichloro acetic acid) | Herbicide - other arable | 2155 | Very soluble (sodium salt) | Fairly persistent Leaches from soil | No inf Probably persistent | Likely to reach water | | (13,22) |
| Triadimefon | Fungicide - cereals | 372 | 260          20 | Degrades to triadimenol which is fairly persistent Not readily leached | No inf Probably persistent | Unlikely to reach water | 10 | (1, 21) |
| Triallate* | Herbicide - cereals | 483 | 4          20 | Fairly persistent Microbial degradation to dialkyl-amine and mercaptan. No inf on leaching | No inf Probably persistent | Likely to reach water | 1 | (7) |

* detected in water supplies at a concentration above 0.1 ug/l on at least one occasion during 1988.

+ since TCA may be formed in water by reaction of organic substances with chlorine, confirmation that any significant concentrations found are due to use of the pesticide, is necessary by examination of the unchlorinated water source.

# Annex 2

**BSI 1988**
BS 6920 The Suitability of Non-metallic products for use in Contact with Water Intended for Human Consumption with Regard to their Effect on the Quality of the Water. British Standards Institution, London.

**Cheeseman and Wilson 1978**
A Manual on Analytical Quality Control for the Water Industry TR66, Water Research Centre.

**DOE 1980**
Lead in Potable Water, Technical Note No 2, Flushing at the Consumer's Tap as a Means of Reducing Drinking Water Lead Levels, Department of the Environment.

**DOE 1984**
Lead in Potable Water, Technical Note No 5, Remedial Water Treatment for Reducing Lead Concentrations in Tap Water, Department of the Environment.

**DOE 1989**
Drinking Water Quality in Public Supplies: an Explanation of the Water Act 1989 and the Water Supply (Water Quality) Regulations 1989.

**HMSO 1976 onwards**
Standing Committee of Analysts, Methods for the Examination of Waters and Associated Materials, London (a series of booklets).

**HMSO 1980a**
General Principles of Sampling and Accuracy of Analytical Results (see also HMSO 1989d).

**HMSO 1980b**
Odour and Taste in Raw and Potable Waters.

**HMSO 1980c**
Ammonia in Waters.

**HMSO 1980d**
Phosphorus in Waters, Effluents and Solid Samples.

**HMSO 1981a**
Colour and Turbidity of Waters.

**HMSO 1981b**
Analysis of Surfactants in Waters, Waste Waters and Sludges.

**HMSO 1982**
Reports on Public Health and Medical Subjects No 71. The Bacteriological Examination of Drinking Water Supplies. (now being revised).

**HMSO 1983**
Permanganate Index and Permanganate Value Tests for Waters and Effluents.

**HMSO 1987**
Code of Practice on Technical Aspects of Fluoridation of Water Supplies, Department of the Environment, London.

**HMSO 1988a**
The Determination of Colour of Waters and Wastewaters; a Supplement.

**HMSO 1988b**
Cyanides in Waters etc.

**HMSO 1989a**
The Water Act 1989.

**HMSO 1989b**
The Water Supply (Water Quality) Regulations 1989, Statutory Instrument 1989 No. 1147.

**HMSO 1989c**
The Water Supply (Water Quality) (Amendment) Regulations 1989 Statutory Instrument 1989 No 1384.

**HMSO 1989d**
General Principles of Sampling, 2nd Edition with Supplements (in press).

**Hunt and Wilson 1986**
The Chemical Analysis of Water, General Principles and Techniques, The Royal Society of Chemistry, London. Second edition 683pp.

**NWC 1980**
Emergency Procedures on Pollution of Inland Waters and Estuaries, Naional Water Council, London.

**WAA 1985**
Guide to the Microbiological Implications of Emergencies in the Water Services, Water Authorities Association, London.

**WAA/WCA 1984**
Actions to Minimise the Effects of Pollution Incidents affecting River Intakes for Public Water Supplies, Water Authorities Association and Water Companies Association, London.

**WAA/WCA 1988**
Operational Guidelines for the Protection of Drinking Water Supplies, Water Authorities Association and Water Companies Association, London.

**WHO 1984**
Guidelines for Drinking Water Quality, World Health Organisation, Geneva.

Printed in the United Kingdom for Her Majesty's Stationery Office
Dd0299145 10.89 C20 488/2 12521